Seasons of a Marriage

H. Norman Wright

Regal Books

A Division of GL Publications
Ventura, CA U.S.A.

The translation of all Regal books is under the direction of GLINT. GLINT provides technical help for the adaptation, translation and publishing of books for mil-
lions of people worldwide. For information regarding translation contact: GLINT,
P.O. Box 6688, Ventura, California 93006.

Trade Edition, 1983
Second Printing, 1984

Published by Regal Books
A Division of GL Publications
Ventura, California 93006
Printed in U.S.A.

Library of Congress Catalog Card No. 82-80010
ISBN 0-8307-0912-6

Contents

Introduction

Before ever starting out on a long journey a wise driver will try to determine what he is most likely to encounter along the way. How are the roads? Will there be any detours? What will the weather be? If he can know some of these things ahead of time he will be better prepared when he gets to a place where his progress could be hampered without this fore-knowledge.

Life is also a journey which has a beginning and some type of conclusion. Its events follow a basic sequence and progression—sometimes smooth and orderly, other times rough and bumpy. Within this journey are stages or periods which might be called seasons. Ecclesiastes states, "To every thing there is a season" (3:1, *KJV*).

Daniel Levinson talks about the meaning of seasons:

There are qualitatively different seasons, each having its own distinctive character. Every season is different from those that precede and follow it, though it also has much in common with them. The imagery of seasons takes many forms. There are seasons in the year: spring is a time of blossoming, winter a time of death but also a rebirth and the start of a new cycle. There are seasons, too, within a single day—daybreak, noon, dusk, the quiet dark of night—each having its diurnal, atmospheric and psychological character. There are seasons in a love relationship, in war, politics, artistic creation and illness.

Metaphorically, everyone understands the connections between the seasons of the year and the seasons of the human life cycle. No one needs an explanation of the lyrics to "September Song." When the hero sings, "It's a long, long while from May to December/And the days grow short when you reach September," we all know that he is referring to the contrast between youth and middle age. When Dylan Thomas in his celebrated poem tells his aging father, "Do not go gentle into that good night," it is clear to all that the coming of night is experienced as the end of life.

To speak of seasons is to say that the life course has a certain shape, that it evolves through a series of definable forms. A season is a relatively stable segment of the total cycle. Summer has a character different from that of winter; twilight is different from sunrise.[1]

Just as there are seasons in our individual lives so are there seasons in a marriage. To know these stages of development ahead of time is to be prepared for them.

Statistics prove that prospects of your having a successful marriage are not very encouraging. I see three reasons why marriages dissolve.

First, one or both persons fail to understand the stages and changes of individual development—the seasons of their marriage—and how these affect their marriage. Second, people have an inadequate basis upon which they build their personal identity and security. The best basis for marriage comes from the one who instituted marriage in the first place, but for many the teachings of God's Word have not been incorporated in depth into their lives to transform both their identity and their security.

Third, some marriages dissolve because the partners were never *prepared* for marriage and because their expectations about marriage were totally unrealistic. David Mace, a pioneer in the field of marriage enrichment, describes this lack of preparation:

> When I try to reconstruct, in counseling with couples, their concepts of the making of a marriage, I find that it adds up to a most confused hodge-podge of starry-eyed romanticism, superstition, superficial concepts, and laissez-faire. Seldom do I find any real understanding of the complexity of the task of bringing two separate individuals into a delicately balanced coordination of each other's thoughts, feelings, wishes, beliefs, and habit patterns.[2]

Why do people marry? What are the underlying subtle reasons for love? What background influences surround the love drive that are somewhat hidden from view?

Both men and women marry to be taken care of. Some view marriage as a safety net into which they gladly fall. We either see or imagine strength in the other person. If the strength is shared and passed back and forth, intimacy can develop. But if the desire of one partner is for "continuous care," growth is limited.

Many actually marry their own physical and emotional need. They have a personal need to be cared for, to be happy, to have economic security, to become a parent, etc. They create an image of a person who they think will be able to meet these needs and then marry their invented image.

Some marry for increased prestige or for personal and professional advancement. Social position, future inheritance, social circles and/or useful and complementary talents sometimes influence the choice of a future spouse.

"Jailbreak marriages" are usually reflective of women although men have been known to use marriage as an escape from their own parents. Marriage under these circumstances usually carries a load of unrealistic expectations. One of the sources of marital conflict is that when people marry they often do not get what they expected to receive—and they receive what they did not expect to get.

When individuals enter their marriage from a deficit position a strain is immediately placed upon the relationship. The spouse becomes the "answer" to unmet emotional needs, love acceptance and happiness. The marriage partner is idealized.

Faults and defects are overlooked or denied.

When couples marry at a young age, they are making one of the most important decisions of a lifetime. But it is being made out of a meager interpersonal experience, facts and awareness of life. There is too much ahead of them and too little behind them. Time and experience are not on their side. So many early marrying couples say later, "I lost out," "I feel as if I have been cheated out of some experience," "I went straight from my parents' home to another's," or "I never had a chance to make it on my own."

Often they lack the maturity and resources to handle the disillusionment and realities of marriage. And not infrequently they break loose during middle age after years of feeling left out. When they do terminate their relationship they often search frantically to fill the vacuum of lost years. One relationship after another is added to the trophy case.

I see marriage as a miniature "body life" concept where man and wife join together to grow toward maturity—through a close, vulnerable relationship—with the ultimate purpose being to honor and glorify God, letting their lives reflect the presence of Jesus Christ. Marriage is a school where we learn to be flexible, to live in harmony with each other, to walk together as one, to strengthen and complement each other as we fulfill our corporate and individual dreams, hopes and ambitions in our journey through life.

In this book we will discuss, first, the stages of marriage—the seasons—you will probably encounter; second, how to find personal identity and security; and third, how to prepare to cope with some of the pitfalls of marriage you never thought about during your courtship period.

Notes
1. Daniel J. Levinson, *The Seasons of a Man's Life* (New York: Ballantine Books, 1978), pp. 6,7.
2. David R. Mace, "Marriage as Relationship in Depth" in *Marital Therapy: Psychological, Sociological and Moral Factors*, ed. H.L. Silverman (Springfield, IL: Charles C. Thomas, 1972), p. 168.

One

In the Beginning

One of the most difficult and complex transitions of life is marriage; paradoxically, becoming a couple is seen as the easiest transition. The couple, friends and family *want* to see it as a happy, joyful time. The new bride and groom may see their marriage as a solution to the problem of loneliness or family hassles; while their parents' response is: "Finally, he's settled down," or "Now she has someone else to take care of her."

Creating Fantasies

As most couples move toward marriage, their sense of reality is distorted by wishfulness and fantasy, and this intense romantic illusion can neutralize the positive development of their marriage. Unrealistic expectations and fantasies create a gulf between the partners and cause disappointments. People can create such detailed fantasies that neither their partner nor the relationship has any chance for survival.

Many marriages today are like the house built upon sand—they have been built upon a weak foundation of dreams. When we dream our minds do not have to distinguish between reality and fantasy, so we are able to create without restraint. Often, therefore, our dreams are starting points for successful endeavors; however, dreams that are not followed by adequate planning usually do not come true.

Marriages built on dreams are risky because dreams do not consider the disappointments and changes that are inevitable in every marriage. When the season changes and the rains of reality and the winds of stress blow upon such marriages, the relationship that *should* hold them together crumbles. Much more is involved in fulfilling dreams than merely expecting them to come true.

Dr. Mark Lee describes this dream process:

Fantasy-making is a form of self-entertainment by which dreamers presume life is made bearable in circumstances which are less than they anticipated. Fantasy is a defense mechanism. Fantasies serve by helping people live with inequities and disappointments. We know that unrestrained thought patterns create larger dimensions for life than human beings can fulfill. Man's inability to accomplish what he can conjure seems less objectionable to him when he creates fairy tales about himself.

The Christian may use imagination for creativity, ending ultimately in the realization of heaven, or he can use it for lesser purposes, even false ones. Imposing blissful fantasies upon a marriage commonly makes for psychological aggression, forcing on a spouse expectations he cannot achieve. Even so, modest fantasies may help marriages, if they are employed to improve legitimate relationships. Fantasies may intensify worthwhile reality experiences. As in so many other matters, fantasies may be blessings or cursings.[1]

Relinquishing marital fantasies is difficult. Often they are such a part of us that their removal is similar to radical surgery.

Negotiating Differences

Building a good marriage means that each person must take time to redefine roles, beliefs and behaviors and negotiate the differences with a partner. Use of space in the home,

time, money, power, family traditions, rituals, friends, voca-
tions are just a few of the issues which will be negotiated. A
hindrance to successful completion of these negotiations is
the factor that one or both spouses might be using the marriage to develop their own identity and improve their own self-
image.

As difficulties arise and disappointments mount, the factor of blame begins to emerge. They can blame themselves or
their spouse, their heritage or their spouse's heritage (e.g., "If
I weren't such a klutz we wouldn't be in this mess," or, "You're
just like your mother"). If this pattern continues the couple
begins to construct a wall between them which further iso-
lates them from each other. They avoid talking about certain
topics which increases their isolation. Monica McGoldrick
describes the process:

A major factor influencing the tightening of couple
relationships over time is the increasing interdepen-
dency of the couple and their tendency to interpret
more and more facets of their lives within the marriage. For example, during courtship, if one partner
becomes depressed, the other is not likely to take it too
personally assuming, "There are many reasons to get
depressed in life; this may well have nothing to do with
me." Such an assumption of not being responsible for
the other's feelings permits a supportive and empa-
thetic response to the other. After several years of marriage, however, this partner has a much greater tendency to view the other's emotions as a reflection of his
or her input and to feel responsible for the other's
depression. After five years of marriage the partner
may think, "It must mean I'm not a good wife, or I
would have made him happy by now." Once each starts
taking responsibility for the other's feelings, there is a
tendency for more and more areas in the relationship
to become tension-filled. Couples then develop a pattern of triangulation in order to avoid areas that
arouse tension between them. Over time they will avoid
more and more areas. For example, if a wife thinks her
husband is depressed because of her, she may feel
inadequate, guilty, and resentful. She may then decide

to become very protective of him and not say anything upsetting for fear of making him feel worse. In either case, the more her reactions are a response to his, the less flexibility there will be in the relationship and the more the couple's communication will become constricted in the areas that are emotionally charged.[2]

Coping with Change

Before we can consider the marital journey we must investigate the individual journey. The concept of a journey is based upon change. We either resist change or welcome it. But we must change if we are going to grow. All changes, whether predictable or intrusive, hold the potential for growth; they are also risky. Untimely or unexpected events upset our plans, their sequence and fulfillment. They bother us because they are *thrust* upon us, leaving us feeling powerless. We don't like to feel out of control and thus we resist, react negatively, or feel overwhelmed instead of seeking creative possibilities in this inevitable situation.

For example, I am a father. I expected to enter the "empty nest" stage of my marriage at about age 48 or 50. And yet at 43—about seven years ahead of schedule—I find myself in that season of life. A son, who was expected to be normal and live with us until college, was born severely mentally retarded. At age 11 he was placed in a home for specialized care. The placement was planned but adjustments still had to be made.

Few things in this life remain stable or permanent. Things change. People change. Relationships change. The unspoken assumption that both the marriage relationship and the partners will remain the same is a prelude to trouble.

Prior to marriage, couples should discuss how they think each of them and their relationship will change. Robert Mason, Jr. and Caroline L. Jacobs have this to say:

Unfortunately, many marriages die prematurely because too many husbands and wives choose to ignore the inescapable fact that people do change.

People can grow apart even when they truly love and care for each other. For some the resistance to change is so deeply ingrained that acceptance of change, even in someone they dearly love, is almost impossible. How-

ever, since it is an indisputable fact of life that people
do change, and since this is one of the major reasons
listed by couples as the source of problems in marriage,
couples would do well to explore in depth their ability
to adjust to the many changes which are inevitable in
the years after marriage.

Difficulties might be anticipated if:

(1) either person seems locked into a way of thinking or behaving which allows for no difference of
opinion or new ideas.

(2) either has communicated to the other what he
or she wants in a husband or wife and gives the
impression that he or she will not tolerate any
deviation from this rigid stance, now or in the
future.

(3) one of the individuals demonstrates a desire to
grow and improve while the other seems determined to maintain the status quo.

(4) one or both show a noticeable lack of curiosity
or interest in the changes which are occurring
around him or her from day to day.

(5) either gets upset easily or acts as if the whole
day is ruined if things do not go according to
schedule or if plans are changed. The individual
who is unable to adjust to change before marriage is not likely to be able to adjust to change
after marriage.[3]

Any new change carries a time of risk, insecurity and vulnerability. But many of life's events can be planned for in
advance—such as having a baby—and can bring security and
satisfaction. Some aspects of the various seasons of a marriage are fairly predictable in the changes they bring. These
also can be anticipated. As a person moves from his twenties
to his thirties, to his forties and fifties he will display characteristics that most people have in common. Becoming parents, having adolescents, the empty nest, the midyears,
becoming grandparents, retirement are seasons we are aware
of; we know when they are upon us for the most part. Some
events, however, come as a surprise and bring tension, pain,
and unexpected circumstances. Loss of a job, illness, birth of

a child with a defect, and sudden death in the family are crises for which one cannot plan.

In their book *How to Stay Married* Clark Blackburn and Norman Lobsenz write:

According to family service experts, any sudden change becomes a threat to whatever marital balance has been achieved. It tends to reawaken personal insecurities that the marriage has successfully overcome or held in check. You've noticed how sick people tend to fall back into childish ways—they become terribly dependent, demanding, unreasonable. Similarly some people regress in other kinds of emotional crises. Long-conquered patterns of behavior reassert themselves, at least until the first impact of the shock has been absorbed.[4]

The normalcy and potential of change is a message which couples need to hear even before they marry. Many relationships could avoid the turmoil and disruption caused by unexpected changes if couples were better informed beforehand. The marital journey is well described by Dr. Mark Lee:

Anyone who has ridden in an old New York subway car will recall his sensation of pitching and rolling as the train raced along work tracks or slowed to a stop in a station. Standing passengers move as one body back and forth with the car's sway and changing velocity. All that prevents a pile-up of bodies on a turn or quick stop are the overhead straps. Almost oblivious to what is happening, passengers grip a strap, automatically tightening and loosening their holds to meet changing situations. In their free hands they hold on for dear life.[5]

Perhaps what we experience in times of change can be likened to a shellfish. A lobster is protected by an extremely hard shell. But as it grows and develops it sheds its old shell to make room for growth. For a while, after the old shell falls off, the lobster is left exposed and vulnerable until a new shell develops.

Hiking in the back country of the Sierras one year, I found myself working along a rock shelf 30 feet above a lake. I was trying to find a way to reach the waterfall at the lake's inlet. At one point—in order to pass around a cliff—I had to relinquish my safe hold on one side of the barrier and almost slither my body across the protruding boulder before I could reach the safety of a new handhold. For a while I hesitated. I didn't want to give up the safety of my grip for the insecurity of moving a few feet, exposed and insecure, to the new location. But to obtain what I wanted, I had to take the risk.

This is often how we feel when we encounter change. But to grow and mature the old must be given up in search of the new. Risk, change and insecurity are positives!

Asked if the love in his marital relationship had changed after 20 years of marriage, a husband replied:

I still feel passion and excitement with my wife. But all of life moves in patterns and cycles, and I think marriages go the same way. A marriage has its dry moments and hot moments, its ups and downs. Most marriages today don't make it. I think the ones that do, survive by going through these changes. As long as you're allowing something to happen within your marriage, then I think there's some chance for its survival. The secret of a good marriage is change. It's gotta move. If it stops, it's dead.[6]

Change in marriage is inevitable. If we view it realistically, we can use it to build positive relationships.

Notes

1. Mark Lee, *Time Bombs in Marriage* (Chappaqua, NY: Christian Herald Association, 1981), p. 16.
2. Elizabeth A. Carter and Monica McGoldrick, eds., *The Family Life Cycle: A Framework for Family Therapy*, (New York: Gardner Press, Inc., 1980), p. 99.
3. Robert Mason, Jr. and Caroline L. Jacobs, *How to Choose the Wrong Marriage Partner and Live Unhappily Ever After*, (Atlanta: John Knox Press, 1979), p. 40.
4. Clark Blackburn and Norman Lobsenz, *How to Stay Married* (New York: Cowles Books, 1968), p. 196.
5. Lee, *Time Bombs in Marriage*, p. 91.
6. Diane de Dubovay and Robert Redford, "Robert Redford," *Ladies Home Journal*, October, 1981, pp. 48,52.

Two

The Season of Expectations

Most marital journeys begin with high romantic intensity. As couples approach marriage they usually have only a superficial awareness of each other's wants, needs and expectation. During this time (and unfortunately for many even after marriage) the least important needs are the ones that get attention.

At the same time, without checking it out with the other, each partner enters marriage assuming that certain events will transpire just the way he or she imagines: "We will visit *my* mother each year on vacation"; "My husband will be home every evening"; "My wife will not work while our children are young"; "We will live in one place and not move around the country," etc. Also the partners imagine that their relationship will develop in a certain way: "We will always be polite to each other"; "My husband will be the spiritual leader in our home"; "My wife will handle the household budget," etc.

Of course, many times these expectations remain unspoken; yet when they are not realized, marital disruption occurs. While most of these expectations are desires—ideal situations—rather than necessities, they still play an important part in marital happiness. What are some of the more prevalent expectations that are nearly guaranteed to go unmet?

Unrealistic Expectations

One of the most common expectations is that *the marriage relationship will always be just the way it was in the early days of marriage*. But change will occur. Unfortunately, it overwhelms many individuals and couples, especially if the change is negative or unexpected.

Another expectation, somewhat related to the first, is that *honeymoon fever can be maintained or recaptured*. But life is not static. The additional tasks and responsibilities of marriage and parenting make this expectation unrealistic. Yet, although the honeymoon excitement wanes, the love experienced later in marriage can be a deeper love.

A third expectation involves narcissistic *mind reading*. "If my spouse loves me, he or she will know what my needs are and do everything he can to meet them." A subtle corollary to this is, "If this doesn't occur, then you don't love me." It would be nice if we were all mind readers, but such an expectation is unrealistic.

Fourth, we demand sameness in our partner: "We should be the same, think the same, do the same things." If the spouse is different something is wrong. However, if we expect our partner to think and act just as *we* think and act, we will quickly become disillusioned. The dissimilarity we observe creates anxiety and insecurity because "If my partner is different, then perhaps I might have to change."

Abraham Schmitt describes the situation this way:

In the midst of the marital struggle the honeymoon dream vanishes, and the despair over the old relationship comes up for reexamination. Suddenly each spouse turns his eyes away from the partner, and looks inwardly and asks "What am I doing to my partner? What is wrong with me? What am I misunderstanding? What must I do to rescue this marriage?" If honestly asked the answers are not far behind: "I really married my wife because of her difference. It is not my job to make her over, but rather to discover and to value that difference. But before I can do that I must accept my difference and I really need her to help me discover my uniqueness. My task is not to mold her into a beautiful vase, but to participate with her to discover that beautiful vase even as we discover it in me. How arrogant of me to think I could shape another human being! How humble it makes me to realize that I need to yield to another and thereby be changed! Our relationship will change both of us—in a process of being shaped into a form far more beautiful than either could imagine."[1]

Demanding sameness in our partner stifles individuality and creates bondage. Only when we give up this expectation can our marriage begin to grow.

Finally, some couples enter marriage *expecting to have problems* because of their differences. Such couples believe that having marital problems is a predetermined fact. They focus on their differences whether or not those differences are really a problem. In such cases they should ask themselves, "What would it be like if I were married to someone just like me? Would I like it?" Who wants to be married to a clone of oneself!

Unfulfilled Expectations

Unfulfilled expectations *generate frustration with anger.*
The higher our expectations, and the more numerous our needs, the more often will we find ourselves blocked. So anger in civilized man is much more often aroused by frustration than by fear. People differ greatly in the amount of frustration they can tolerate, but all of us have a flashpoint at which we experience a surge of anger. In marriage . . . this can easily happen, because we find ourselves in a situation in which expectations are high, and frustration can often occur. We would venture the opinion that for normal people, being married probably generates more anger than any other interpersonal situation in which they normally find themselves.[2]

A further result of unfulfilled expectations is that they eventually *evolve into demands.* One spouse senses the

demanding tone in the other's voice and is offended by it. To
help define these expectations try stating them in the form of
a demand. Write them down or share them verbally with your
spouse. A husband's demands might be: "I demand that you
get up first and cook my breakfast." "I demand that you always
be home when I arrive after working all day." "I demand that
you dress the way I've suggested in order to please me."

A wife's demands might be: "I demand that you work
around the house every Saturday." "I demand that you spend
time with the children." "I demand that you become the spiritual leader in the home."

Dr. Joseph Maxwell describes the negative effects of such
demands:

> Most of us are unaware of the demands we make on
> our spouse to exhibit certain traits or behaviors. What
> we are aware of is the feeling of anger or annoyance we
> experience when we are frustrated in realizing our
> demands. The feeling is so strong, so dependable, so
> apparently autonomous that we think it is not only jus-
> tified, but unavoidable. We believe that the feeling is
> caused by our spouse's failure rather than our
> demand. This occurs because we are very aware of the
> failure but are largely unaware of the demand which
> designates the failure as a bad event.
>
> Demandingness is a formidable barrier to marital
> growth because the person doing the demanding is
> likely to spend most of his or her time and energy
> catastrophizing and pitying self, and to spend little cre-
> ative energy in planning ways to develop the relation-
> ship. Since every behavior of a spouse necessarily
> evokes a responsive behavior from the other spouse,
> such personally upsetting behavior as is produced by
> demandingness will usually have significant effects on
> the actions and feelings of the partner. In most cases,
> when one partner reacts negatively the other one
> responds by behaving equally negatively, creating an
> endless cycle of demandingness that leads away from
> growth and development of the relationship.
>
> If only one spouse is willing to give up his or her
> demandingness, the cycle can not only be stopped, but

reversed toward strengthening the marriage.[3]

What happens internally to a person whose demands are not met? The sequence flows something like this: A wife makes a demand of her husband but he does not meet it. She then becomes angry because she believes he "should" or "ought" to do what she demanded. (It is not he, but she who generates the anger.) Every time he fails to respond to the demand she says to herself, "It is awful." She then feels anger toward him and self-pity toward herself. Each time he fails to meet her demand, her emotional responses become more intense.

Unmet Expectations

When your expectations are unmet how can the problem be resolved? Of course one way is for your spouse to give in and work harder to meet your needs. But this does not always happen, nor should it if your demand is unrealistic. Another solution which can greatly lessen the frustration and anger is for you to *change* your expectations of your spouse.

To do this, first identify and write down those expectations of yours which have developed into demands. Then define and list the additional areas in which you have expectations. Now submit the demands and expectations to these questions:

1. Do we both have expectations in this area?

2. Do I have the same expectations of myself as I do of my spouse? Why not?

3. How are our expectations of each other alike or different?

4. Whose expectations are stronger?

5. Whose expectations are most often met? Why? Because that person is older, stronger, more intelligent, male, more powerful?

6. Are my expectations more worthy of fulfillment than my spouse's?

7. Where do my expectations originate? From parents, books, church, siblings, neighbors where I grew up?

8. Do all the people I know have the same expectations in a given area?

9. Do I have a "right" to my expectations?

10. Am I obligated to live up to my spouse's expectations?[4]

One way to reduce demands is to challenge them to see if they are rational or realistic. Ask yourself the following additional questions for each demand:

1. Is this expectation I have of my spouse supported by objective reality? Is it objectively true that he or she should act this way?

2. Am I hurt in any way, shape or form if this expectation is not fulfilled?

3. Is this expectation essential to the attainment of any specific goal I have for my marriage?

4. What does this expectation do to my spouse's perception of me?

5. Does this expectation help me achieve the kind of emotional responses I want for my spouse and me in marriage?[5]

If you answered no to the first question and to at least two others it is obvious that this expectation is invalid. If any demand or expectation is valid, then approach your spouse in a new manner, such as: "I would appreciate it if you would . . ." or, "I would really prefer that you . . ."

Another way a couple can evaluate their expectations of each other is to each list 20 of your expectations of your partner. Then write on a sep rate sheet of paper a two- or three-line paragraph about each expectation. The paragraph should tell how your own life and your marriage will be effected if that expectation is never met. Then exchange your lists of expectations, but not the paragraphs. Now each person has an opportunity to look at and to evaluate each expectation. You can respond to each expectation by making one of the following statements:

1. "I can meet this expectation most of the time, and I appreciate knowing about this. Can you tell me why this is important to you?"

2. "I can meet this expectation some of the time, and I appreciate knowing about this. Can you tell me why this is important to you? How can I share with you when I cannot meet this so it would be acceptable to you?"

3. "This expectation would be difficult for me to meet for these reasons. Can you tell me why this is so important to you? How will this affect you? How can some adjustment be worked out?"

By going through this evaluation a couple will probably be talking about these issues in detail and in a rational, constructive manner for the first time.

Meeting unfulfilled expectations is essential for a person's satisfaction and development. It is necessary for both husband and wife to analyze their needs and their wants in order to determine which are realistic and which are not. Sometimes people confuse their needs with their wants.

In most cases when a couple enters marriage, each person is demanding little but receiving much. Under the influence of very intense feelings, each responds to the other's needs. But in time this changes. More demands are now made on each of them from the outside, whereas previously most of the attention could be focused on their partner. As outside demands increase, we tend to meet less of our spouse's needs in order to fulfill more of our own needs. The couple moves into the stage of giving less and expecting more and unfulfilled needs become a source of conflict.

One writer describes the problem this way:

To be able to balance one's own needs along with all that is required of one, to remain attuned to another's needs, to be able to give when one feels more like getting, to be able to protect one's own interest, all these require a certain level of maturity, that is, a resolution of the various developmental tasks along the road to adulthood that may not have been completed. Thus, many individuals who enter marriage are often looking for a way to resolve unmet needs and are handicapped in their capacity to give. The normal stresses of a changing relationship affect these people more intensely.

The other fact should be mentioned because of its frequent occurrence. The very characteristics that are the most appealing initially and that pull the couple together inevitably become sources of major irritation later.[6]

Sometimes the unmet need is for security or attention. Some people are raised in an atmosphere of neglect which deprives them of needed attention. Because of this they may feel that they are not very important. They may be unable to be concerned with the feelings of others. Instead they run from one person to another, hoping that each person will give them the attention they need. They are perpetually dissatisfied with their relationships with others, including their spouse.

There are times in marriage when their need for attention is fulfilled but soon the emptiness returns. They long for a deep, intimate relationship; but what they are really looking for is a parent. They have an excessive need for warmth, love, and attention. If their spouse tries to get close to them, they become fearful that if their spouse truly knew them intimately he/she would not like them. Paradoxically, they are unable to accept the very attention they need. They place unrealistic demands upon their partner to fulfill their needs and tend to see their partner as someone to be used.

There is no way that any one person can meet all the wishes of another. Desires and needs accompanied by the notion that one deserves to have what one wants must be acknowledged for what they are: archaic feelings and wishes from the past which impede realistic expectations in the present. Once spouses can accept this, one can stress the importance of diversifying ways in which each spouse gains satisfaction, lest they be overly dependent on each other and accrue resentments. This is not to say that they should not expect some of their desires to be met; expectations that some needs be satisfied are both legitimate and appropriate. The difficulty is when expectations exceed realistic possibilities (and this, of course, varies with spouses). The persistence of infantile fantasies presents major, and sometimes insurmountable, obstacles to achieving mutuality in the relationship.[7]

How We Tend to React

Every couple brings unique characteristics and perspectives into their marriage. But some common themes and frustrations occur. One of the main frustrations involves blocking the fulfillment of each other's psychological needs. Both husband and wife may be involved in a destructive pattern of response which drains the other's self worth. Each downgrades the other which creates a fight/withdraw pattern. Each tries to convince the other of his "rightness" and hopes this will "straighten out" his partner. Each spouse may insist that the majority of responsibility for marital problems rests with his partner.

The issue may not be who is right or wrong, but what is the best way of responding to each other. The reason they are at this point in their marriage is that they have not yet learned to relate to each other effectively.

Couples need to see how they are mutually frustrating to each other. All people have needs: the need to feel worthwhile and the need to be liked and accepted by others; to feel self-respect and self-appreciation, among others. When these needs are met we are contented and satisfied. And each of us then is better able to help our partner feel worthwhile and likeable.

When our essential need for self-esteem is unmet, we begin to feel unworthy. And we find it difficult to share our good feelings and sense of worth with our spouse. Instead we set up a blaming pattern manifested by rejection, ridicule, and the tendency to nag.

The result of this behavior is that we feel even more unlikeable and worthless. We begin to defend ourselves through a process called the "fight-flight" pattern. We *fight* or attack our spouse as much as possible and in as many ways as possible. Most fights include blame, criticism, and put-downs.

After the *fighting* comes the second stage, *flight*, often referred to as a "cold war." We withdraw to feed our own feelings of hurt and rejection and probably begin to plot ways of inflicting more hurt upon and downgrading our spouse.

There are many ways to withdraw. Some retreat into silence and refuse to speak to their partner. Some withhold sexual intimacy. Others retreat into their jobs where their business success builds their self-esteem. Their excessive absence becomes a retaliation against their partner. Others escape into drinking or drugs. Still others find another person who appears to appreciate them and who sees them as a worthwhile person. Each of these patterns continues to frustrate the other partner until it becomes a vicious circle.

The vicious circle pattern, which is common, can be seen with this illustration. A man under pressure at work stops at a bar with his friends for a couple of drinks before coming home. He lets the time go by and arrives home an hour and a half later than usual. His wife, who has been waiting for him, has strong feelings. She is frustrated because he didn't call and let her know, and feels rejected and worthless because he came home so late. He spoiled her dinner and all her hard work. So she verbally attacks him. He doesn't like being attacked because it makes him feel worthless and unacceptable. He becomes resentful and may shout at her as he walks out the door without eating dinner.

Later that week or the next, the pattern is repeated. He stops off for a couple of drinks and enjoys the atmosphere and acceptance he feels in the bar. It's better than that nagging wife waiting at home! She feels further neglected and uncared for as she realizes that he would rather be with his friends than at home with her. So she attacks and blames him even more. And the vicious circle continues.

On Sunday he decides to play an early morning round of golf but promises his wife that he will be home in time to take her to the 11:00 church service. But after the game he goes into the clubhouse bar for a drink or two with his golfing partners. The time slips to 11:30. She calculates where he might be, calls the bar and has him paged. She then berates him over the phone in the presence of his friends.

Embarrassed to think that some may have sensed what was occurring, he wants to prove that he is not dominated by his wife. He suggests another game of golf and does not return home all day. This is a mutually self-destructive pattern which each of the partners is feeding.

It is not unusual for couples to develop such vicious circles. The result is that the harder each tries to deal with a problem, the worse it gets.

Each person is emphasizing his own needs rather than the results of his actions. The more a wife nags and reminds her husband that the house needs painting or the garage needs cleaning, the more he seems to procrastinate.

It is possible for a couple to break this negative behavior pattern if each of you is willing to submit to a very definite and specific program of action. Each spouse must identify his responsibility for his half of the problem. It will take time and work. But if what you are doing now is not working, then you have absolutely nothing to lose.

The way to break the pattern is for each person to describe how the mate's behavior makes him or her react. When the two explanations are put together each person may tend to become defensive. No one wants to hear that his own behavior is making his spouse behave in a negative manner. Therefore it is important for each one to do his own analysis of the situation separately.

Here is a procedure which Dr. Carlfred Broderick of the University of Southern California suggests:

1. By yourself and in writing identify a problem between you and your spouse which meets the previous criteria of a vicious circle. That is, the harder you try to deal with the problem, the worse it gets.

2. From your point of view describe what your spouse does or does not do that makes the problem worse.

3. Now write out in detail what it is that you do or fail to do either in response to what your spouse does or as an effort to change him.

4. You probably have some expectation in mind as to what your spouse's response ought to be to what you do in number 3. What had you hoped he or she would do?

5. What has been your spouse's actual response to your actions or words?

6. What are your feelings about that response?

7. What keeps you from trying something new? What do you fear would happen if you tried something new? If you are on the receiving end of a request, why do you resist and how? What would happen if you responded favorably to the request? Is the request really the problem, or is there a power struggle occurring? How do you resist? Many people use what is called passive-aggressive behavior. These include forgetting, withdrawing, neglecting, ignoring or withholding. And these are just as effective as a direct, outwardly angry or critical remark.

8. Write down at least two or three new responses that you could make. List a possible positive response on the part of your spouse to your positive change. It will be easy to think of a negative response ("She'll never change"), but this only

wastes energy and cripples progress. List only positive responses. If you will act "as if" your partner is going to change in response to *your* positive change, there is a greater likelihood the vicious circle will be eliminated.[8]

It is important for a couple to see how they set up the vicious circle. Each person's behavior, and the consequences of that behavior, need full and careful exploration. As each person begins to see what his behavior is triggering in his partner and what a different response may do, then the cycle can be broken. In many cases changing the *way we act* even without full insight into the problem can lead to the discovery of a better way of relating. Part of the process of marital growth is to discover more effective ways of responding to each other.

Changing the Way We Act

Two of the most important ingredients in a marriage are (1) the way in which each person behaves toward the other, and (2) the feelings those behaviors generate. Therefore, what improves a marriage is how we change our response to these behavior patterns.

In order to change our behavior we need to discover where our behavior patterns come from. This will help us know how our marriage got where it is today.

What occurs between a husband and wife is not random behavior. People *decide* to behave the way in which they do. It is interesting to note that behavior exchanges are often developed by mutual UNSPOKEN consent. Couples are aware of the effects of their action upon the other. It sounds strange, but we tend to *accept* both the positive and negative behavior of our partner. You might say, "You mean if my spouse continually criticizes or nags me or puts me down, I am saying that it is all right for him/her to do that?" Yes, that is correct. We agree to the negative behavior of our spouse in many ways. Complaining, withdrawing, being passive—all of these can be a means of cooperation.

If your spouse manipulates you, the manipulator could not be successful if you did not cooperate. If a husband nags and his wife constantly receives the brunt of the nagging, she is actually encouraging him to nag. Each is receiving some sort of satisfaction from this interaction. And each is involved in a power struggle. Otherwise one would be willing to admit that his behavior is not that effective and make some type of a change.

Why do couples continue with behavior each of them basically dislikes? There are numerous reasons. *Pride is a big factor.* If each person feels that he has been wronged, then both will hesitate to be the first one to take steps which might improve the relationship. Or each may feel that the spouse will see a positive move as a sign of weakness. Or changing behavior can present a feeling of anxiety. To try something new involves the risk of failure. Something new is uncomfortable even though the old may be painful and self-defeating.

Some do not initiate change because they lack the skill, motivation or creative thought it takes to have *positive expectations*. This also involves lacking the ability or fortitude to imagine and define what a better relationship would actually be like. Using imagination and fantasy as a motivational means of moving in a positive direction is a vital force. The Bible describes it: "As a man thinks in his heart so he is" (see Prov. 23:7). The way in which a person visualizes or anticipates events has much to do with the way they turn out. If you believe that an upcoming event is going to be successful, your approach to it including your speech, posture, poise, determination, etc. will reflect this. And in turn your attitude will affect the others around you. If you expect to have an accident when you drive on the freeway you will be more tense, awkward, lower in perception, and generally more prone to actually have an accident.

By having positive expectations, your behavior assists you in creating a positive outcome. If you are willing to make positive changes in your relationship and behave *as if* there will be a positive outcome, there is a much greater possibility of success. It may very well free up your partner to make positive changes as well.

One way in which to increase positive behavior in a marriage is to start having regular "caring days." Ask each other the question, "What would you like me to do for you to show how much I care for you?" The answer must be positive, specific, something that can be performed daily. The purpose of each action must be to increase positive behavior, not to decrease negative behavior. "Please greet me with a hug and a kiss" is positive. "Don't ignore me so much" is negative. "Please line the children's bikes along the back wall of the garage when you come home" is better than "Please train the children to keep their bikes in the proper place." It is better to avoid the subject of a recent conflict because neither spouse is very likely to give as easily on these. Avoid making vague comments by writing down beforehand your answers to the question, "What would you like me to do for you to show how much I care for you?"

These requests should, as much as possible, be something only your partner can fulfill. If they are things that a hired hand could perform they may create problems. For example, if they are mostly task-oriented like "wash the car," "take out the trash," "clean out the camper," "have the dishes and house all cleaned up by the time I get home," etc., they do not reflect intimacy and the cultivation of a personal relationship. Some better responses would be, "Ask me what excites me about my new job," or "Turn out the lights and let's sit holding hands without talking" or "Rub my back for five minutes."

Each list should include 15-18 items. Listing as many items as 18 creates more interest and makes it easier to follow through with requests. When you each give your list to your spouse the only discussion you may carry on about the list is to ask for clarification if it is needed. Now it will be your commitment to do at least five items each day on your spouse's caring list, whether or not he or she is doing any of the positive behaviors on your list.

Here are some suggestions for your "caring" list:

1. Greet me with a hug and a kiss before we get out of bed in the morning.

2. When you are out walking, bring back a flower or a leaf.

3. Look at me and smile.

4. Call me during the day and tell me something pleasant.

5. Turn off the lights and light a candle when we have dinner.

6. Ask me how I spent my day.

7. Meet me at the bus stop sometimes as a surprise.

8. Tell me how much you enjoy having breakfast with me.

9. Tell the children (in front of me) what a good parent I am.

10. When we sit together, put your arm around me.

11. When we are together at home, ask me what record I would like to hear, and then play it.

12. Wash my back when I'm in the shower.

13. Have coffee with me in the morning before we wake the children so that we can have a five-minute talk together.

14. Hold me at night just before we go to sleep.

15. Ask my opinion about world affairs after we watch the news.

16. For no special reason, hug me and say you like me.

17. Hold my hand when we walk down the street.

18. When you see me coming up the drive, come out to meet me.

19. Put a surprise note in my lunch bag.

20. When we're together, end your sentences with "dear" or "sweetheart."

21. When we part in the morning, blow a kiss to me.[9]

The basic principle behind this approach is this: If couples will increase their positive actions toward each other, they will eventually crowd out and eliminate the negative. The consequences of behaving in a positive way override the negative. In addition, behaving in a loving, caring way will generate a more positive response on the part of the partner and can build feelings of love.

By doing this activity you will, first, experience the important "I must change first" principle; second, you will build in yourself and your spouse both self-confidence and other-confidence; and third, you will begin to anticipate improvement in your relationship. Because people anticipate improvement they tend to behave accordingly.

Another approach of increasing positive actions toward each other is the positive application of specific passages of Scripture. The phrase "one another" is repeated numerous times in the New Testament. These admonitions, if put into daily application, will bring a radical change to your marriage. Read the list I have prepared below and do one of two things: (1) take the list and write out your own application of each verse, then commit yourself to at least a weekly demonstration of each principle (many will be applied daily); (2) as a couple ask each other, for each passage, "In what way would you like me to apply this passage toward you?" In doing this you gain a greater insight into the needs of your spouse.

Principle	*Application*
John 13:34—Love one another.	
Galatians 6:2—Bear one another's burdens.	
Ephesians 4:2—Bearing with one another (forbearance).	
Galatians 5:13—Serve one another.	
Ephesians 5:21—Be subject to one another.	
Philippians 2:3—Thinking more highly of one another.	
Ephesians 4:32—Be kind to one another.	
Romans 12:10b—Show honor to one another.	
1 Thessalonians 5:11a—Encourage one another.	
1 Thessalonians 5:11b—Strengthen and build up one another.	

Increasing positive behaviors is a practical application of the Word of God. Time and time again Scripture admonishes us to behave in a positive manner:

Ephesians 4:32: "And become useful and helpful and kind to one another, tenderhearted (compassionate, understanding, loving-hearted), forgiving one another [readily and freely], as God in Christ forgave you." (*AMP*)

Colossians 3:12,13: "Clothe yourselves therefore, as (God's own picked representatives,) His own chosen ones, [who are] purified and holy and well-beloved [by God Himself, by putting on behavior marked by] tenderhearted pity and mercy, kind feeling, a lowly opinion of yourselves, gentle ways, [and] patience—which is tireless, long-suffering and has the power to endure whatever comes, with good temper." (*AMP*)

Notes

1. Abraham Schmitt, "Conflict and Ecstacy—Model for Maturing Marriage," an original paper.
2. From *How to Have a Happy Marriage* by David and Vera Mace. Copyright © 1977 by Abingdon. Used by permission.
3. Nick Stinnett, Barbara Chesser and John DeFrain, eds., *Building Family Strengths: Blueprint for Action* (Lincoln, NB: University of Nebraska Press, 1979), p. 112.
4. Ibid., pp. 118,119.
5. Ibid., pp. 117,118.
6. Billie S. Ables, *Therapy for Couples* (San Francisco: Jossey-Bass Inc., Pubs., 1977), p. 3.
7. Ibid., p. 218.
8. Carlfred Broderick, *Couples* (New York: Simon and Schuster, 1979), p. 103, adapted.
9. William J. Lederer, *Marital Choices* (New York: W.W. Norton and Company, 1981), p. 63.

Three

The Season of the Twenties and Thirties

We are a people who dream. We have a lifelong pattern of imagining. We dream of the type of person we will become, the type of marriage we will have and the type of parent we will be. And we use these dreams to measure whether we are a success or failure. These dreams or images come from both childhood and adult experiences, and a major adult adjustment is to refashion our dreams to fit reality. If we as adults cling to these dreams in the face of a totally opposite reality we may experience disappointment, rage, depression and turmoil.

Adulthood is a dynamic changing time for men and women. You are different today than you were five years ago. What will you be like five years from now? Ten years from now? What will you be doing? Who will you be? What do you want to be at that time? If you could know the answers to these questions now it would make the future easier.

While we cannot tell you everything you may experience, this chapter gives a preview of some of the more prevalent situations you may expect during your twenties and thirties. The question is, "How will these experiences affect my future life?" If you are already past this season of your life then you will identify with some of these occurrences and can see how they are affecting you presently. The transition of the forties are a reflection of the influence of the two previous decades.

We begin the venture into adulthood as we are released from adolescence, usually in our twenties. Hopefully, our parents have completed the deparenting process and we are free to move into a new stage of independence and responsibility. For some the move from adolescence to adulthood is like a major earthquake with dramatic upheavals and shifts in personality. For others the transition is less traumatic. No matter how the change occurs the young adult should be in a somewhat steadier, more integrated state than he was in his teens.

Early adulthood is a time of either giving up some past relationships or changing them. Beliefs and dreams have to be altered. Childish fantasies begin to dim, although a certain idealism continues to motivate us. In a sense life becomes narrower and more focused.

Some pressing decisions must be made during early adulthood which involve time and energy. Our inner motivations and the outside world both pressure the fledgling adult for decisions. These decisions include:

1. Should I attend college or seek employment?

2. If I go to school what courses should I take?

3. Can I handle work and school too? What about the pressure?

4. Who pays the bill if I go to school? (This could perpetuate dependency upon your parents.)

5. After college, what? Employment or graduate school?

6. What about a relationship with another person? Should I pursue casual dating, serious dating or marriage? Or should I wait a while?

7. What will I miss out on because of any of my choices?

8. What do I really want to do that would be a reflection of me as a person? Who am I and how should this be expressed?

9. What will give me the greatest security? What will create the greatest insecurity?

10. What is God's will for my life?

Questions such as these continue and continue. We become increasingly aware that wrong choices can bring lasting consequences. The childhood belief that there is no time limit is over.

The great task of the twenties is really "What do I do with this period of my life?" Choice is the screaming theme. Dr. Daniel Levinson of Yale labels this time period "The Dream." During early adulthood the adult attempts to make his dream become a reality, and by his own choice. It is not a peaceful time, as Maggie Scarf suggests:

> The newly emerged self of the early twenties can, nevertheless, be compared to a relatively recent geological formation. It is patently there, and has its own contours and outline; it has its dimensions, height, circumference, and breadth. Still, it is subject to underground shudders and tremblings; it is newly formed and not settled; it can still shift in its shape and its structure. It may still experience great aftershocks. For, whether or not the adolescent transformation has been perceived as a time of earth-shaking alterations, it has—as earthquakes do—involved the release of accumulated strains and pressures at the very core of one's being.[1]

A person in his twenties is beginning to formulate his dream or vision of what he wants in life and to pursue it. He is building his life structure. Some people are foresighted; they are able to lay meaningful foundations for their future. Others are quite shortsighted—there is still a vagueness about their dream.

One way to bring a dream into focus is to ask yourself, "What kind of a life do I want to lead as an adult?" This can turn a vague fantasy into, as Levinson describes it, "imagined possibility that generates excitement and vitality."[2]

Two Primary Dream Pursuits

What is your dream? Two major dreams that adolescents formulate are (1) the vocational dream and (2) the marital dream. Your main task during your twenties is to clarify and define your dreams and then develop a plan to attain them. Some questions you may ask yourself are: "Where does the will of God enter in?" "What does He want for me at this particular time of my life?" "Where does 'Seek ye first the kingdom of God and His righteousness' enter in?" (see Matt. 6:33). "Am I seeking a vocation or my future spouse in order to *establish* my adequacy or out of a *sense* of adequacy?" And perhaps most important, "Does this dream come from within me or has it been forced upon me?" This last question is particularly critical in your choice of a vocation.

Some people pursue a vocational dream because of economic factors, lack of other opportunities, the wishes of parents, a desire to please a fiancée, personality defects or even because they possess a unique talent which could become an occupation. Whatever the reason it is possible for you to go into an occupation, be very successful, and yet be bored and discouraged. Many people in our country are in this position.

Pursuing a wrong dream in your twenties and building your life around it will bring consequences you must live with for many years. Your marriage and your total outlook on life will be affected by the choice and pursuit of your vocational dream. However, it is well to remember that the vocational choices you make now are not necessarily irrevocable. Change at this point and in the future is usually possible.

When the time comes for you to pursue your dream you may do one of two things. First, because you want to get the whole thing over with and you feel that you will have a firm, secure future, you may make some strong, definite commitments that are virtually set in concrete. In doing this you may overly resist and feel threatened by change or intrusions from the outside. If you do not take enough time to carefully consider your choice of occupation, however, you will encounter frustration in the future. You will feel locked in and restricted. It is as though a person were building a very straight, predictable railroad toward a destination and, at the same time, he erects a wall on both sides of the track, eliminating all alternative directions.

The other tendency is to continue to explore and experiment without a definite commitment. Although this gives you the opportunity to change directions more easily, if this exploration continues throughout the twenties, you may turn into a vocational transient. Some people make numerous changes in vocation, relationships and residences, but there must come a time of settling down.

In a sense the person in his twenties must walk a tightrope between exploration and settling down. It is interesting to evaluate your own particular pattern as it is reflected in other areas of life besides your vocation. In your man/woman relationships, your spiritual life, and in other areas, are you rigidly set or continually open to change?

There is no guarantee about your choice of occupation. Those who make the commitment too early may learn to live with regret. Those who delay their commitment or never commit themselves at all lose much of the satisfaction of personal fulfillment.

Also during the twenties most commit themselves to marriage. As it is in choosing an occupation it is in choosing a spouse: a person often makes his choice before he is ready to know exactly what he wants and how to achieve it.

What happens if you marry at the start of your transition from adolescence to adult? You find yourself learning to separate from your parents, trying out the new adult world and adapting to a spouse all at the same time. Sometimes early marriage (ages 17-22) perpetuates difficulties with parents and you end up retaining some of your childish qualities. The new husband and wife may both feel extra strain at this time because they are both emerging.

He or she may have had little experience in forming peer relationships with members of the opposite sex. The mate may become a tool to help the person relinquish his or her relationship with parents and become an adult.

If you wait to marry until you are between the ages of 22 to 28, being married can either contribute to or detract from your personal development. Your marital partner should be a person who will share your dreams and who is willing to let you share his or her plans and dreams.

However, if you reach your thirties and still aren't married you may experience pressure from friends, parents, and even business associates to marry; and you may feel compelled to do so. You may try to conform and make your life "normal" without having resolved some of your inner conflicts.

No matter at what stage a couple experiences marriage there will be issues and conflicts to resolve. Both the man and woman must continue to develop personally as well as together. They can no longer rely upon their society, culture, family or even their commitment to their faith to keep their marriage together. Marriages receive less outside support today than they used to because of the change in values, culture, divorce laws, and an emphasis upon selfishness and individualism. Greater effort and commitment on the part of each are needed. Greater commitment to the fidelity and permanency concepts of Scripture is also needed.

A lasting relationship is more possible if both partners continue to grow and develop. If the husband uses his wife to further the attainment of his dream, and in the process she loses her own dream, her growth will be stifled and eventually both will be disappointed. Or a medical student marries and his wife supports him for years in the pursuit of his dream. She foregoes her own advancement, education and intellectual development. Soon the children arrive. He is into his eighty-hour-a-week practice and becomes acquainted with a woman who is freer, less restricted and more intellectually stimulating than his wife. He decides to change partners.

Or a man may choose to marry because a family man is more acceptable in his profession. In this case he may see his wife and children as necessary accessories. Or sometimes a marriage relationship may become a hindrance to the pursuit of a man's dream. His wife may have no interest in his dream and may even prevent him from attaining it. Her own dream may be complementary, different or antagonistic. Any of these conditions could affect the success of the marriage.

If a woman sees herself in the traditional roles of wife and mother she may derive her identity from her husband and what he does. She sees her husband as her protector and turns her whole being over to him. She continues to support *his* dream as long as he gives sufficient attention to her and their family, and as long as she feels needed by him and their children. She probably believes that men are attracted primarily to physical beauty and helplessness. But as she ages, her physical attractiveness may fade, and her husband may grow weary of her "helplessness." By her thirties and forties she may be needed less and less by her husband and family and she may be forced to seek out her own identity.

If a woman has been overly dependent on her husband and

decides to change, her husband may feel threatened, especially if the change costs him something. He accepts it better if it benefits him. She could begin to believe that her husband is the obstacle to her own growth. In actuality it may just be that he is not giving her the encouragement she desires from him.

It is not uncommon for a woman in her late thirties or early forties to experience an identity crisis. She may become disillusioned with her traditional role; she may resent her caretaker husband. If she decides to develop some independence and pursue a career she may face a number of obstacles. Job availability may be limited. Or if she finds a job she may find the role of both a career woman and a homemaker a strain. Some women are a bit fearful of the feelings of competition and power within them which have lain dormant for so many years. Accepting these and using them in a creative way, both within the home and in a career, can be a freeing experience.[3]

But no matter what age a person chooses to marry, he or she will find certain problems—as well as a great many advantages—in becoming adjusted to married life.

Marriage in the Early Years

In the midst of developing their own personal lives a man and a woman marry. The romantic idealism eventually turns to the question, "Will we make it together?" Great expectations and hopes are mixed with fears, anxieties, and surprises. A host of new and unexpected events come into their lives. Those which are expected or anticipated will be handled fairly smoothly but the surprises can be disruptive. This is why extensive and thorough premarital preparation with a minister or counselor is such a necessity. As there are stages and phases to work through in one's own life there are also important stages and phases to work through in the first few years of marriage. Consider some of these and reflect now upon your own marriage.

The first task is to define what a "wife" is and what a "husband" is. It is important that each retains his/her individual identity while drawing close together as a couple. A marriage relationship is meant to be a freeing-up relationship and never a confinement. Each person is freed-up to develop uniqueness and spiritual giftedness in his or her own way, and join these with the other in a marital relationship to give it strength and greater potential. This may mean breaking loose from preconceived images each one has of what a wife or husband should be. If couples cannot allow each other to develop and grow and be creative in defining new roles, the conflict will be intense. As one author so vividly puts it, "both of you will wind up drilling holes in your own marriage before it has left the shore."[4]

A second task is to create a new relationship with your parents. You need to be independent from them yet retain a close, loving relationship. You must break the parent-child ties and reestablish them in an adult-adult relationship. A person needs to complete the separation process from his parents for a marriage to develop. One must "leave" in order to properly "cleave" as it states in Genesis 2:24. By having made peace with one's parents and separating completely, a man/woman can be at peace with his/her self and thus with a marriage partner. If the "leaving" has not successfully occurred in your marriage I would suggest additional reading in the following books: *Your Inner Child of the Past* by Hugh Missildine, and *The Indelible Family* by Mel Roman and Pat Raly.

A third task is to develop romantic love of courtship into a love based upon steady commitment. Before you married you were drawn to your friend because of a specific character trait. You saw it as a strength. But now that you're married you want him or her to change because it has begun to bother you and you see it as a weakness. It is an expression of his or her personality. If it bothers you it needs to be discussed but not attacked as a weakness. Labeling a behavior as a weakness does little to bring about a change.

The love which is needed to stabilize a marriage is the type of love which God displays to each of us—an unconditional commitment to an imperfect person. This takes energy and effort. It means caring about the other person as much as you care about yourself. Mel Krantzler describes what marital love actually means.

Marital love requires the ability to put yourself in your partner's place, to understand that the differences that divide you are the differences of two unique personalities, rather than betrayals of your hopes and dreams. The unconditional willingness of each of you to understand and resolve these differences through the sharing of your deepest feelings, concerns, attitudes and ideas is a fundamental component of marital love. Postponement of your need for instant gratification when your partner feels no such need; sharing the struggle to triumph over adversities as well as sharing the joys and delights of being together; nurturing each other in defeat caused by forces beyond our control and renewing each other's courage to prevail in the face of despair; carrying necessary obligations and responsibilities as a flower rather than as a hundred-pound knapsack; acknowledging the everyday value of your partner in a look, a smile, a touch of the hand, a voiced appreciation of a meal or a new hair style, a spontaneous trip to a movie or restaurant; trusting your partner always to be there when needed; knowing that he or she always has your best interests at heart even when criticism is given; loyalty and dedication to each other in the face of sacrifices that may have to be made—all of these are additional components of marital love that courtship knows little about.[5]

These are just a few of the tasks a couple faces in the early years of their marriage. Beginning a family is another challenge.

Beginning a Family

The arrival of a baby marks the beginning of a new family structure and even a new marital outlook. The novice father and mother establish new patterns of behavior, discover new joys and suffer new stresses. They begin to notice greater uncertainties and fears. Parenting is risky.

Many family study experts say that the birth of the first child is a major crisis for many couples. Why? Because they probably spent more time preparing to get their driver's license than they did preparing for parenthood. Most couples have only a vague idea of what is entailed in the task of parenthood let alone the changes which occur in the marital relationship. One of the biggest adjustments is how to integrate this new person into the family so all three lives are enhanced. There is one guarantee that a child brings with his or her arrival: the guarantee that his or her presence will NOT bring instant happiness or solve marital problems. A child is a bottomless pit of needs and demands. Often a couple will see their child as an enemy because of their own frustration and inability to cope with these changes.

Being a parent is like being an astronaut. No matter how much you are told, how much training and instruction you receive, your own experience can't be predicted: It will be an uncharted course.

And parenthood is like swimming. Some people plunge in without thinking and do a beautiful backstroke; others barely manage a "survival float"; still others can't do even that. They have to call for help.

The birth of a child tests the identities of both parents. Husbands and wives by this time have found ways to build their identities through success in certain performance-oriented tasks, jobs, or skills. When the child arrives, the qualities they feel they possess are soon tested. If they are successful in this new venture, they are satisfied that they made a wise decision. But if either the results are negative or their anticipated needs are not fulfilled through parenthood, their identity may suffer. If they depend on positive feedback concerning their role as a parent and it doesn't come, their self-esteem may begin to diminish.

Responding to a child is different from responding to adults in the career world where there are definite and specific guidelines for communication. There the end result of communication in many cases is immediate and there is equal and free communication. When a child is involved, especially a very young child, there is little direct communication. A parent's confidence in knowing how to handle situations can erode.

Picture yourself in the bind of many formerly employed mothers. You had a degree of independence and accomplishment in your job. Now you have exchanged your job for motherhood. Often you feel insecure and indecisive in your new role. You receive little assurance that what you are doing is best. The feelings of competence you had when you were employed diminish, and your ability to accomplish anything may seem to diminish also. Thus your identity begins to erode. The husband's support and involvement definitely must act as a stable force during this time.

Having a child has the effect of making a woman become selfless and more concerned about the care of another than she was before. To some degree she must rely more on her husband than she did before. As she takes care of another, she needs to be taken care of herself, whether she wants to be or not. In a healthy relationship this need has little or no lessening effect on one's sense of identity.

The new role of motherhood often does away with some of the wishes and desires she can no longer pursue. "Abandon yourself for the good of another" is the maxim she has heard from her parents, church, or friends. Following this advice she encounters conflict; for in not meeting her own needs and wishes sufficiently, she has less to give to the child and her fear of being a "bad mother" intensifies.

When you dream about children and being a parent you fantasize about yourself and your child to be. You dream about the type of parent you want to be and the type of child you want to have. Fantasizing is normal; but are the images you see in your dreams realistic? Are they grounded in realistic expectations or are they only wishful thinking? Do these dreams help you fulfill your own desires?

Most couples who experience any preparation at all for parenthood do so minimally during the nine months of pregnancy. And most mothers do more reading and discussing than fathers.

We spend many years preparing for our vocation and in some instances work into it gradually. We spend six months to four years becoming acquainted with our spouse prior to marriage and this relationship gradually grows and develops. Not so with parenthood! We are aware that the child is coming, and then abruptly—a minute later—this new stranger is alive, loud and demanding.[6]

There are numerous challenges to meet. It is important for both a wife and husband to see the child for who he or she is. The child is not a sexual rival nor a substitute for either spouse. Each spouse needs to develop flexibility to meet his partner's needs in a new way. Expanding the ability to express frustrations, feelings, and even delaying some need-satisfaction will be a major step. Realizing that the initial draining schedule of a newborn does not last forever will help you keep things in perspective.

Pregnancy is the time for the creation of new images. A couple begins to think of themselves as "an expecting couple." They learn to accept the pregnancy which involves starting to accept a new role. When a baby arrives the couple begins to form an attachment to the child. This is a process which occurs over time. As the child grows the parents learn to accept the responsibility of being an authority. They must also become teachers and resource specialists for their children, which continues throughout the teen years.

The task of parenting becomes more complex because of three additional factors: (1) each parent is going through his own individual growth and change process; (2) the couple is working out their own relationship; (3) if there is more than one child, parents have multiple parental roles.

For example, with one child you move through various stages such as accepting the pregnancy, becoming the parent of a two-year-old, a four-year-old, a six-year-old, an eight-year-old, etc. With one child, a parent proceeds through his own adjustments progressively one step at a time. But now add a second child when the first one is four years old. Now the parents are parents of a newborn and a four-year-old—two roles at once. Four years later, the third child arrives. Now the adjustment involves an eight-year-old, a four-year-old and a newborn. It is true that the second or third child is easier because we now have some experience behind us, but difficult because attention, time and energy are divided.

Discovering Your Identity

During his twenties a man continues to search for adequate paths toward the fulfillment of his dream. As he progresses, he usually finds a mentor (one who influences, teaches and guides him) or even a series of them. This is usually someone who is older, experienced, somewhat protective—a combination guide, companion, father figure. At this time he is also looking for the woman who he assumes will be his partner and share his dreams and visions. During this time between the twenties and thirties there is consistency and orderliness.

Do women follow this pattern? Is there orderliness and consistency in their lives as well? In one study it appears that women tend to do more shifting and changing during this time and their lives are less predictable. Women actually have more options open to them from marriage and motherhood to a career. Many women after a few years of marriage and mothering become restless and want to enter the career world, but they often find roadblocks in their path.

On the other hand, some women who have established themselves in their career during their early twenties at about thirty move into marriage and mothering. They do so with a strong and definite commitment to this new phase. Their desire to have a child is strong. Some women have expressed the feeling that they continued to feel somewhat like children until they had become wives and mothers.

Do women seek out mentors as men do? It appears that women who marry and establish a family during the early twenties do not look for a mentor. It could be that their dream of marriage and a husband fulfills their adolescent hopes. Many women see themselves as an addendum, a support, and her energy goes into relationships with husband and children. She helps her partner pursue his dream rather than searching for one of her own. In some fashion her identity becomes involved in her husband and his pursuit.

Career-oriented women tend to seek out an older, more experienced mentor.

Some women who marry early eventually begin to think of pursuing a dream of their own, having already helped their husbands pursue their dreams.

The twenties, therefore, no matter which direction is taken, is the time for the searching and discovery of identity.[7]

How do men and women accomplish this? Is there a difference in the way they search for identity? Women have a strong tendency to find their source of identity or self-esteem in intimate relationships. The key word here is *relationships*. Men's striving to complete their dreams is more individualistic. One means of finding their identity is through their occupation.

Some have suggested that it is only after a woman has achieved a sense of worth and security with her partner that she gains security about her personal value. It also appears that her emotional attachment gives her the security to branch out into other life goals. Some of these goals may be nontypical, nontraditional and competitive, but now they can be approached quite freely.

The Two-Career Family

When there is economic strain the marriage is a prime target for the never-enough-money conflict. The job becomes the prime concern. It is becoming more common for both husband and wife to work. In 1980, in more than 19 million U.S. families, both husband and wife were breadwinners. For many it takes two paychecks just to survive economically. Many of these women do not have adequate skills for a well-paying job so they find a job that is dull and routine. They worry about being laid off if they are unskilled or if there is a recent hiring. They still discover biases against them as women in a number of professions. And a rat race of competition in some companies.

In many families both partners *choose* to work. They are career-oriented rather than job-oriented. Many women are not completely fulfilled by the role of wife and mother. They have skills for which someone (probably parents) invested 30 to 40 thousand dollars for four years of college. And now they are crying to be used. Even in the professional field for women there are problems as well as benefits.

Some women attempt to develop themselves in both work and marriage simultaneously. This can heighten a woman's inner tensions considerably, for the role expectations are opposite in these two areas of life. For example, what would happen in the career world if the woman were warm, emotional, expressive, noncompetitive, supportive? What would happen in her marriage if she were controlling, pushing, self-assertive, competitive, dominant, etc. This sometimes happens as it is often difficult for her to shift roles. She has to create two different lives at once! Many decide that it is better to remove themselves from one of these roles. She either quits her job or her marriage. Men do not encounter this problem because they are expected to exhibit the *same* characteristics in both marriage and occupation, so their tension and ambivalence are less.

Although the economic burden may be lightened if both partners work at their chosen careers, problems can arise. One of the biggest problems for two-career families is, who does the housework? One husband, whose wife also worked, began to keep track of the family's use of time. He discovered that he spent an average of 45 minutes a day doing household chores. Their two sons spent 15 minutes a day and his wife spent six hours every evening. Each had his own set of complaints about the time allotment. The outcome was that the husband and sons took on a much greater share of the household chores to the satisfaction of everyone.

There is one positive potential available if a husband would take advantage of it. Because his wife is also working he does not have to moonlight. Therefore, he can spend more time with his children and create deeper bonds with them. A father must be involved with his children. In fact, Scripture has more to say about the role of the father than the mother. By intimate involvement with his children he can learn to be a more caring and sensitive person. A husband committed to his wife cares and encourages her and is more likely to share household duties. But most men do not become that involved at home with or without children. The stress of shuffling chores may be more than he expected. If the husband refuses to help, resentment and distance soon appear in their relationship and they begin to reinforce each other in a negative manner. Soon their commitment is to their career rather than to each other and their marriage. The husband's desire as to whether she remains a housewife or is employed outside the home is a major factor. If he approves there is likely to be higher marital adjustment than if he disapproves.

With both the wife and husband employed outside the home, marriage is a challenge. To maintain the relationship in a loving, close manner will take constant effort. The response to the following questions can help you decide whether or not you are responding constructively to this challenge. Even if one of you works at home and the other one away, answer as many of these questions as are applicable.

Do you tell each other what happened during your working day?

Do you really listen and care about what has happened to your spouse on the job?

Does only one person ask or tell the other?

Do you refuse to share your concerns about your job because you think your spouse won't understand the problems you are facing at work?

Are you too embarrassed to tell your spouse that your boss reprimanded you, or that you are terrified about making a presentation at a company meeting?

Do you try to put yourself in your spouse's shoes and understand that what might prove to be no problem to you might be a great problem to your partner, requiring your helpful feedback?

Do you admire your spouse's strengths on the job as you would a colleague's, or are you secretly envious that he or she possesses those qualities?

Do you feel you are entitled to a greater say in family economic decisions and in household management because you are earning more money than your spouse?

Do you really like the fact that your husband/wife works?

Do you take pride in your wife's professional competency for her sake as well as your own?

Would you secretly like it better if your wife greeted you at home every evening with a clean house, refreshments and a hot dinner?

Do you really do your full share of the housework without continual prodding from your wife or without feeling argumentative and resentful because you feel you are always getting the short end of the stick?

Do you view helping your wife entertain her clients as important as her helping you entertain yours?

How would you feel if your wife made more money than you? If she already is making more money, do you have mixed feelings about that fact? Do you talk to her about your feelings?

Do you feel that you are in competition with your husband regarding who has the best job and who makes the most money? If you are, is the feeling one of healthy competitive-ness as in a track race, or a feeling of guilt or anger because you are competing with him?

Do you do more than your fair share of the housework rather than hold your husband to his end of the bargain because you don't want to make waves?

If your husband is making a larger salary than you, do you feel guilty when you spend money on yourself because you believe you are spending "his" money?

Do you allow your husband's purchasing desires to take priority over your own because he makes more money than you do?

Do you feel you are entitled to less decision-making power in your household because your husband makes more money than you do?

Do you label the total income you and your husband make "our" joint income, or do you regard the earnings of each of you separately as a measure of the power each of you brings to your marriage?

How would you feel if you made more money than your husband? If you are making more money than your husband, do you feel guilty or secretive about sharing that fact with friends?

Do you consider your wife's/husband's job a "safety net"? How would you feel without it?[8]

Today there are numerous life-style options available for a woman from which she can choose. Her own mother probably didn't have much choice; her role was already written in tradition. The dilemma today for women is, "Am I making the right choice?" And this question sometimes haunts them. They feel inward pressure based upon a mixture of beliefs of what a "good mother" is. Pressure comes from friends, church, inter-pretation of Scripture, parents and other sources. But the internal personal questioning of whether she is doing the right thing may be the greatest plague.

Part of the dilemma comes from the inward screaming of two sets of needs. For example, many women earlier in their lives have the need to develop the career part of their personal-ity. Once this is established the need of the nurturing mother comes to the forefront. Both needs are normal but how does she handle both? Is she to give up one for the other? Can she fulfill both at the same time? A parent who works is no less a parent than one who is at home constantly. With a supportive and encouraging husband, careful planning, and proper selection of child care many couples do work out this type of life-style.

If both partners work because of economic necessity or a career choice they need to resolve their own attitudes. Guilt and questioning must be put to rest so they can give themselves to their tasks with all their energy in a positive way. They also need to learn to handle spoken and unspoken disapproval from outsiders, and even to occasionally challenge outside reaction.

Couples today need greater freedom in their choice of a lifestyle than they did 50 years ago. Roles and pressures have changed. The myths of children becoming delinquent and marriages ending in divorce at a greater rate when the mother is employed are just that—myths. The facts do not support them. As I counsel young couples preparing to marry I wonder how they will make it financially today without both being employed for some part of their marriage. They are not seeking a standard of living that is lavish and unrealistic—they simply want to survive.

We all know of couples where both work or have a career and it has created problems. There are many pressures and problems to work through when they have children. But many make the adjustments quite well.

One young couple I know has chosen a shared career marriage. Both have taught school for ten years. They have two young children. Both parents arrive home between 3:30 and 4:00 each day, have two weeks off at Christmas and a week off at Easter. They have the summer off together because of their profession and they have two salaries. The children in this home actually have much more time directly involved with their father than in most other families.

A woman sought me for counseling because of her struggle with working and being a "good" mother. She loved her job as a kindergarten teacher and had a definite influence in the lives of her pupils. The family also benefited from her salary. But she was struggling with doubts: "Am I neglecting my children? Shouldn't I be at home with them during the day?" We analyzed her present schedule and discovered a number of factors.

1. She spent much of her present time at home with her children in a creative manner.

2. One child was in school already and returned home when her mother did.

3. The youngest who was in a preschool would attend preschool anyway whether the mother worked or not. The parents felt the socialization the child received there was valuable. If mother were at home the child would be gone until 12:30, return home for lunch and then nap from 1:00 until 2:15. The outcome was that by being at home the mother would gain possibly an additional four hours per week with the youngest daughter and no additional time with the oldest.

Couples must consider the positives and negatives in their own situation, then they must decide carefully for their own lives, not to please outsiders.

The Thirties

The thirties is an interesting time period for most individuals. Earlier in their lives many women operated upon the false assumptions that "life is simple and controllable" and "threats to my security are not real." By their thirties they have discovered that this is not true! The flaws and limitations of the twenties still need to be refined in the thirties. Dissatisfactions begin to cramp them. Many times people in their thirties would like to make some changes in their lifestyle, but new directions and change can be threatening.

Around the age of 30 many career women decide they also want a marriage. They have proved their value and worth in the business world and now the search for something more begins. This "something more" for many is a child. Becoming a mother is now a desire rather than something to dread. They see it as yet another source of fulfillment.

If having children has been postponed until this time there will be new adjustments in time, economics and the marriage relationship. Some husbands may want very much to start a family at this point; others will see it as a threat to their freedom, their standard of living and their marriage.

At some point in their thirties most men do want to make some type of change. They want to create something more satisfactory for the balance of their early adult life. Life is becoming more serious and they begin to think, "If I am going to change my life, I had better do it now before it gets too late!"

One of the questions which both men and women ask at this time is "What's missing in my life that I want to change?" When have you last asked that question? What is missing in your own life? What needs to be done to fulfill your life? To give your life greater meaning?

One of the most significant questions which needs to be asked again and again is, "In what way is the presence of Jesus Christ making a difference in my life?" In many cases our relationship with Jesus Christ is an addendum to the rest of our existence. We have responded to Him but have not invited Him to be a participant with us in our personal and marital life.

This is a time for career commitment to deepen. This may mean a deeper commitment to an established profession or commitment to a new one. Commitment carries with it two opposite feelings—security and insecurity. Security in the sense that a career has been chosen; insecurity because in so doing one has to give up experimenting with other job ideas. Adventure has been sold out to security.

Quite often change and commitment come about gradually. This was my own experience. At 27 I began to teach graduate school part-time while I was serving full-time in the ministry. Then at age 30 I resigned my position at the church and went full-time into the field of teaching. It was a smooth transition, moving from involvement in Christian education in the church to teaching the same subject to others. I attempted to hold on to the previous position for a while in a part-time capacity. But I soon discovered that it would not work. The church expected full-time performance and so did I, which was impossible. So I quit my part-time involvement. The life structure which had been built in the twenties provided a groundwork for my change at 30.

There are other men who experience this transition as a major crisis. If they find their present circumstances intolerable, they may experience chaos and loss of hope for the future.

The majority of men tend to find this a stressful time of life. A man may feel like he is swimming from one island to another, past the island of the future. He is afraid he will be stuck in the middle and drown.

In the marital relationship there is a greater desire for intimacy but equally as strong is a desire for space. Some feel smothered by too much closeness but yet want intimacy. A desire to run away in one form or another is not uncommon.

Many men and women return to educational pursuits to enhance a career or to begin a new one. But the desire to begin to back off from work and enjoy life more is also present.

Toward the end of the thirties a man moves into a period referred to as "settling down." He now pours himself into whatever is most important to him, whether it be his occupation, family, friendships, etc. It is interesting to note that most men follow a similar pattern. But they are not always aware of what they are actually seeking or doing until someone points it out to them. If you were to ask most 30- to 40-year-old men, "Do you realize that at this point in life you are giving yourself to whatever is most important to you? Did you realize that you are establishing yourself in society? Do you know that you are trying to become more competent in what you do? Do you realize that you have a very strong goal orientation at this time?" some would say, "Oh, I don't know. I just do what I do." Others might say, "I hadn't thought about it in that way." After analyzing what they are doing they begin to realize, "Yes. I guess I do fit that pattern. No one ever spelled it out for me like that but that seems to be what I'm doing." Being consciously aware of what one is doing allows the person to be in greater control of choices. It also allows a man or a woman to consider what God would have them do with their future.

After all of this comes middle age. Where are you in this vignette of the twenties and thirties? Is it yet to come or has it been? What will be the results and what have the results been? We all seek stability, fulfillment, identity and adequacy. It doesn't come from work, relationships or parenthood. It comes from who God is, how He sees us, and what He has done for us. Allowing God to have a prominent place in our lives will ease our striving and give us meaning. "Seek ye first the kingdom of God and all these things will be added unto you."

Notes

1. Maggie Scarf, *Unfinished Business* (New York: Doubleday and Company, 1980), pp. 218,219.
2. Daniel Levinson, *The Seasons of a Man's Life* (New York: Ballantine Books, Inc., 1978), p. 71.
3. Material in this section was adapted from both Scarf, *Unfinished Business* and Levinson, *The Seasons of a Man's Life.*
4. Mel Krantzler, *Creative Marriage* (New York: McGraw-Hill Book Co., 1981), p. 50.
5. Ibid., p. 54.
6. Adapted from Marvin N. Inmon and H. Norman Wright, *Preparing for Parenthood* (Ventura, CA: Regal Books, 1980).
7. Scarf, *Unfinished Business*, adapted from p. 225.
8. Krantzler, *Creative Marriage*, pp. 67-73. More information on this subject is in *The Two-Career Marriage* (Philadelphia: Westminster Press, 1980); Caroline Bird, *The Paycheck Marriage* (New York: Rawson, Wade Publishers, Inc., 1979).

Four

The Season of Mid-life

I believe that middle-aged marriage, lived as it should be and can be, offers qualities that nothing else has ever superseded: A shelter where two people can grow older without loneliness, the ease of long intimacy, family jokes that don't have to be explained, understanding without words. Most of all it offers memories."[1] Mid-life can be a time of reminiscence, growth, challenge, delight—a time to welcome.

For some couples this description is a reality. But for others mid-life is a time of crisis. Turmoil occurs in the marriage because of personal changes taking place within the husband or wife or both.

At middle age the normal defects in any relationship seem to show up in sharper focus. When the children leave there is more time to notice and confront each other. The buffer and distraction of children are no longer present. Often the romance and passion of the earlier years are gone, the adhesive which is very much needed but is so difficult to generate once again. Now the couple are faced with the fact that they are getting older and the threat of aging is painful.

This crisis time at middle age is also the time for what Ken

Kesey described in his novel *Sometimes a Great Notion* as the "go-away-closer disease." The husband or wife may be starving for contact with the spouse but avoids contact like poison when it is offered. He or she may long for human relatedness but ends up sabotaging any chance for it to happen. He or she may erect barriers to keep the other from getting too close, too intimate, too involved—yet the person is unhappy and restless in isolation.

How does one catch this strange go-away-closer disease? It seems to come in varying degrees with the middlescent malaise. The anger, frustration or disappointment we feel about the world and what it has done to us (or prevented us from doing) is directed at the person with whom we live in closest proximity. It is another form of "kicking the cat." We may sense that things have gone awry, but for some reason we find it impossible to talk about the situation with our spouse. Eventually we stop ourselves from caring about, or doing as much for, our spouse because our own problems require all of our attention. It is hard to be sensitive to the needs of our spouse if we are locked in our own inner struggles. Besides, since we think no one else really understands us, we must keep our defenses up lest we reveal more than we want to show. Who wants someone else knowing what we are really like down inside—the resentments, the hurts, the frustration, the failures?

Intimacy is lost, also, as spouses begin to see each other's faults more glaringly. Over the years faults may come to loom larger as virtues turn into vices, and eventually they become blatantly intolerable. Here again, spouses usually show a reluctance to discuss the unpleasant aspects of each other's personalities—except, perhaps, in the heat of anger when they shoot out derogatory terms that question their partner's sanity or intelligence.[2]

What Is Middle Age?

What is middle age? It is a time of life which ranges anywhere from age thirty-five to the mid-fifties. It is also a state of mind; as a person senses the passage of time his values and view of life begin to change. It is a time when he comes face to face with fulfilled and unfulfilled dreams, achievements, goals, and relationships; with middle age comes the opportunity to develop potential and take on new challenges and direction. It is also a time of great responsibility; business decisions, family decisions, community and church decisions and responsibilities all weigh upon the person in this prime time of life. It is a time of realizing potentials and accepting limitations.

Funny but true! (Or too true to be funny?) Middle age is:

—the time when a man is always thinking that in a week or two he will feel as good as ever—*Don Marquis.*

—when you are too young to get on Social Security and too old to get another job.

—when you're sitting at home on a Saturday night and the telephone rings and you hope it isn't for you—*Ogden Nash.*

—when you stop criticizing the older generation and start criticizing the younger one.

—when your old classmates are so grey and wrinkled and bald they don't recognize you—*Bennett Cerf.*

—when [you] are warned to slow down by a doctor instead of a policeman—*Sidney Brody.*

—when you want to see how long your car will last instead of how fast it will go.[3]

Mid-life Crises for Men and Women

Mid-life can be a time when marriages quake and break. During this time men and women change and so do their relationships. The change may be slight or massive. Isn't it interesting that a man will dump his wife for the reason he first desired her? He wanted her to be supportive, dependent, stable, a homebody; he now finds her dull, frayed, too conventional. He has grown in one direction and she another. A chasm has developed.

Many men by mid-life have made a heavy investment in hard work. Now for the first time they begin to count the cost. They have pushed ahead on the basis of myth, only to discover that work will never be able to deliver them from all they wished.

A number of studies indicate that at mid-life a reversal occurs. Men tend to move toward passivity, tenderness and intimacy which they previously repressed. They move toward more expressive ventures and goals. Women tend to become more autonomous, aggressive and cognitive. They now seek more instrumental roles such as a career, money, influence.

During mid-life the issue of identity comes to the forefront for many women. The question, whether cried aloud or whispered, is, "Who am I?" Many women have spent most of their lives doing what others wanted them to do and fulfilling others' needs. They have also fulfilled certain expected roles whether they fit those roles or not. Many have led a life of conformity and regression. Some of the messages which many women heard over the years have led to this identity confusion. Messages like, "Achieve, but not beyond what is appropriate for a girl"; "Strive, but be careful you don't damage your chances of marriage"; "Be smart, but don't overshadow the boys, just enough to impress others."

One part of the woman moves ahead to achievement, one part retreats. One part moves forward, the other holds back. And then the day comes when a woman asks, "Why? Why should I not be me?"

Many a woman exists through her husband—she has been represented by another person. Finally she decides that a vicarious identity is not sufficient and she begins to resent his being her caretaker. Often a woman begins to believe her husband is the obstacle to her growth. He may or may not be the blockade; it may be he is failing to give her the encouragement she needs. If she wants a career now she may face a number of obstacles—job availability may be limited because she has been out of the job market for an extensive time; trying to meet the needs of a job and homemaker can create too much strain; she may fear her feelings of competition or power which have lain dormant for years. However, accepting these and using them in a creative way within both home and career can be a freeing experience.

Also emerging at this time is the male *mid-life crisis*. Jim Conway, in his excellent book *Men in Mid-Life Crisis*, describes the situation:

The man approaching mid-life has some strange

and difficult times ahead of him. He may negotiate the walk along the unfamiliar top of the brick wall with little trouble, but many men in mid-life feel more like Humpty Dumpty.

The mid-life crisis is a time of high risk for marriages. It's a time of possible career disruption and extramarital affairs. There is depression, anger, frustration and rebellion. The crisis is a pervasive thing that seems to affect not only the physical but also the social, cultural, spiritual and occupational expressions of a man's life.

It is a time when a man reaches the peak of a mountain range. He looks at himself and asks, "Now that I've climbed the mountain, am I any different for it? Do I feel fulfilled? Have I achieved what I wanted to achieve?

How he evaluates his past accomplishments, hopes, and dreams will determine whether his life ahead will be an exhilarating challenge for him or simply a demoralizing distance that must be drearily traversed. In either case, he is at a time of trauma, because his emotions, as never before, are highly involved.[4]

For some men, mid-life becomes a war zone with numerous enemies. *One such enemy is his body.* It no longer responds as it used to for it's slower and perhaps sagging. His body doesn't look as good nor does it have the stamina and energy it once did. Gaining too much weight becomes an increasing problem.

The war intensifies because of the second enemy—work. Trapped—nowhere to go—bored and in financial bondage. He may have a prestigious position but he feels there has to be something more fulfilling than this. Or maybe he is on a treadmill to nowhere in his position.

Strange as it may seem, the third enemy is his family. Again, he has this feeling of entrapment. If it weren't for the financial obligations to the family he could quit his job. He thinks about living off the land, or traveling. But the pressure of braces for tee⁺h, tuitions for Christian schools, the mortgage and other financial demands from his wife and children press upon him.

Daniel Levinson has pioneered the research regarding the

mid-life time. Here is his practical description of this time in a man's life:

Some men do very little questioning or searching during the Mid-life Transition. Their lives in this period show a good deal of stability and continuity. They are apparently untroubled by difficult questions regarding the meaning, value and direction of their lives. They may be working on such questions unconsciously, with results that will become evident in later periods. If not, they will pay the price in a later developmental crisis or in a progressive withering of the self and a life structure minimally connected to the self.

Other men in their early forties are aware of going through important changes, and know that the character of their lives will be appreciably different. They attempt to understand the nature of these changes, to come to terms with the griefs and losses, and to make use of the possibilities for growing and enriching their lives. For them, however, the process is not a highly painful one. They are in a manageable transition rather than in a crisis.

But for the great majority of men—about 80 percent of our subjects—this period evokes tumultuous struggles within the self and with the external world. Their Mid-life Transition is a time of moderate or severe crisis. Every aspect of their lives comes into question, and they are horrified by much that is revealed. They are full of recriminations against themselves and others. They cannot go on as before, but need time to choose a new path or modify the old one.

Because a man in this crisis is often somewhat irrational, others may regard him as "upset" or "sick." In most cases, he is not. The man himself and those who care about him should recognize that he is in a normal developmental period and is working on normal mid-life tasks. The desire to question and modify his life stems from the most healthy part of the self. The doubting and searching are appropriate to this period; the real question is how best to make use of them. The problem is compounded by the fact that the process of reappraisal activates unconscious conflicts—the unconscious baggage carried forward from hard times in the past which hinders the efforts to change. The pathology is not in the desire to improve one's life but in the obstacles to pursuing this aim. It is the pathological anxiety and guilt, the dependencies, animosities and vanities of earlier years, that keep a man from examining the real issues at mid-life. They make it difficult for him to modify an oppressive life structure.

A profound reappraisal of this kind cannot be a cool, intellectual process. It must involve emotional turmoil, despair, the sense of not knowing where to turn or of being stagnant and unable to move at all. A man in this state often makes false starts. He tentatively tests a variety of new choices, not only out of confusion or impulsiveness but, equally, out of a need to explore, to see what is possible, to find out how it feels to engage in a particular love relationship, occupation or solitary pursuit. Every genuine reappraisal must be agonizing, because it challenges the illusions and vested interests on which the existing structure is based.[5]

Who is the last enemy in mid-life? God! Often He is viewed as an unfair God. He is blamed for the bind that the man finds himself in. God is responsible for the aging, the bodily deterioration, the terrible job, the urges and drives. God is seen as a tyrant or a killjoy. The man either has forgotten or never knew who God really is. God is not the enemy, Satan is. Jesus said, "Any one who enters in through Me will be saved—will live;" and this means physical life as well as spiritual. "He will come in and he will go out [freely], and will find pasture. The thief [Satan] comes only in order that he may steal and may kill and may destroy. I came that they may have and enjoy life, and have it in abundance—to the full, till it overflows" (John 10:9,10, *AMP*).

God is not the enemy; He is the provider, the helper, the deliverer, man's friend.

Phases of Adjustment
During mid-life there are several phases of adjustment.

One is a shift from placing value upon physical ability to greater valuing of wisdom. There is a natural decrease in physical strength, stamina and youthful attractiveness. Powers of judgment, however, are increasing and thus become a natural substitute. Making wise choices becomes a valued substitute.

There is also a shift from thinking about one's partner as a sex object to greater appreciation of him or her as a companion. Each person becomes valued now for new reasons.

During this time it is important that we be emotionally flexible. This means sometimes shifting emotional investments from one person to another or from one activity to another. As our own parents die, our children leave home, or death takes other significant people of our own age, we must form new emotional attachments within the bounds of propriety, or emotional impoverishment can occur.

We must work at remaining mentally flexible or we may develop a hardening of our mental arteries. Because we have worked so hard to develop a number of answers to life and perhaps to achieve some status, we may tend to be more rigid mentally.

If we know of the possible physical and mental pressure of middle age it may ease its passage. A mother experiencing menopause may have strong feelings about the ending of her reproductive capacities. She may worry about the possibility of being no longer sexually attractive. If she has an adolescent daughter she may feel threatened by her daughter's developing sexuality. Both of them are likely to experience varying mood swings as one menstrual cycle is in the throes of development and the other is leaving. The daughter's fears may center around her newly developing femininity and womanhood while her mother fears that these elements are vanishing. If the mother's dreams and aspirations have been frustrated they may be imposed upon her daughter. Similar conflicts and uncertainties may also exist between father and son.

All family members, whether adolescent, young married, middle age or elderly, are affected by past memories, perceptions of the present and anticipation of the future. The adolescent has few past memories and is anxious to move quickly toward his fantasies of the future. He isn't very eager to learn from the storehouse of memories his parents or the elderly have, for they hold little fascination for him.

The middle-aged man has numerous memories, some hidden because of pain or disillusionment. As he sees the fresh eagerness of the emerging adolescent, he is reminded of earlier dreams and desires. Some of his dreams were realized and some were not. He is very much aware of the present realities of life and may tend to caution the youth or try to bring a sense of reality to his dreams.

Many middle-aged couples feel caught in a vise because of tensions between the generations. The adolescent is trying to gain entrance into the adult world and be recognized as such. If grandparents are also present, they are in the stage of resisting being thrust out of full recognition in the adult world. Both pressures add to the already present sense of threat the middle-aged couple is feeling because of where they are in their own adult development. As they see their own parents aging they see what life will be like for themselves in a few years. They are at a midpoint with about as many years left in the future as they have used up in the past. The elderly have just a short future, an uncertain present, and a very long past.

Because of these phases of adjustment there is a tendency toward increased marital stress at this midpoint in life.

Causes of Male Mid-life Crisis

The term "male mid-life crisis" literally means changes in a man's personality. These changes usually occur rapidly and are substantial, thus appearing both dramatic and traumatic.

A mid-life crisis can take varied forms. The most common form is called the "goal-gap mid-life crisis." This refers to the distance a man perceives between the goals he has set for himself and the achievements he has actually attained. It is a gap between what a person hoped to accomplish and what he has actually done.

We live in a very highly educated society with more men involved in white-collar jobs than in blue. Because of our high level of education, more expectations are placed upon us. The more we know, the more we should be able to use our knowledge creatively. But there are limits to career opportunities.

There are ceilings and most often these ceilings are reached during mid-career. For many, a mid-career and mid-life crisis hit at the same time.

When a man hits a plateau in his career it can be an unsettling experience. If his work is the foundation of his personal identity, the questioning involved in the mid-*career* crisis can shift into the mid-*life* crisis. Because so much of a man's status and life meaning comes from his career accomplishments, he feels that he really has no more meaning than his title. Personal identity is defined by work.

Many of his individual goals are called into question at this time; career and material goals are some of the most common. Material goals are often a standard by which a person measures his career goal. How he perceives his present and future ability to meet these material goals can help to bring about mid-life crisis. Moving into the best neighborhood, joining a prestigious club, or sending the children to an exclusive school may be goals which, if unattainable, indicate failure—a devastating experience. The typical response to this goal gap is, "I've been cheated out of something that is rightfully mine." It could be money, a life-style, a position, an advancement, etc.

Goals vary among individuals but responses to blocked goals are quite similar. Men attempt to alter the goal-gap difficulty in various ways:

1. They may simply set aside their goals and withdraw from their pursuits. They may do this through careful questioning and reevaluation or through an angry reaction.

2. They may continue the pursuit of the goal with increased effort either within the same company or another.

3. They may revise their goals and stay in their career area.

4. They may change to another career which gives a better opportunity to attain the desired goals.

These changes are not always simple or easy.

Dr. Michael McGill says:

It does take courage for a man to give up in mid-life what he's been doing and to get after his goals in another career arena. Many men find it easier to live with being less than they had hoped to be than to run the risk of possibly falling short of their goals a second time. For others, the realization of a goal gap spurs them on to greater efforts at goal achievement in the same arena. Without changing their aspirations or their chosen avenue for achievement, these men respond to the goal-gap crisis of their middle years with renewed commitment, as though challenged by their goal shortcomings. The changes in the personality and behavior of these may be as dramatic as the changes seen in men who choose other responses to the goal gap.[6]

It is all right for us not to realize some of our dreams. God may have a better idea for us according to His plan and purpose. Second Chronicles 6:7-9 is an example of changed plans. King Solomon is dedicating the temple which he has constructed. He states, "Now it was in the heart of David my father to build a house for the name . . . of the Lord." However the Lord counseled David, "You did well that it was in your heart. Yet you shall not build the house." (*AMP*) David had a dream and a project. Yet it was actually his son whom God chose to fulfill the dream.

You and I have dreams also, but there are many which will never be completed by our own hands. Others may be able to take the dream from within our heart and make it a reality. God may say to us as He did to David, "You did well that it was in your heart."

It is important for a man, at some point in time, to take an inventory of his goals and his identity. He needs to thoughtfully answer questions such as:

1. Do my goals have meaning for me at this time of life?

2. Do my vocational goals or my occupation give me identity and meaning in life?

3. Are my goals realistic and do I have the ability to attain them?

4. How do my goals relate to the Word of God?

5. What is the goal that I have for my life five years from now in the following areas of my life: (1) vocational, (2) spiritual, (3) marital, (4) family, (5) recreational?

Some men experience a career crisis because of another reason: they *have* attained their goals. Some may be satisfied and fulfilled, others say "So what?" or ask "Is this all there is?" They wonder what this dream attainment really means now and for the future.

Men experiencing the mid-life crisis seem to draw attention. Books are written about them and by them. But what about the man who sails through this time period without any serious trauma? What do these men do that keeps them from experiencing a crisis? How do they respond to the same events and experiences that devastate some of their peers?

One factor is that their identity is not threatened by the events of mid-life. They have multiple sources of identity and are thus less vulnerable to a loss. Men who find various ways of defining who they are have greater stability. But they must do this early in life. Attempting to achieve this stability when the crisis occurs is often difficult.

Many men, though, do find their identity threatened by events during middle age. How is it possible to make these events constructive and productive?

Resolving Potential Crises

There appears to be a pattern which many middle-aged men follow in order to successfully resolve potential crises. Each man needs to determine what each of these steps means for him and how he can take them. He may need examples of how other men have taken these steps.

The resolution pattern involves the following:[7]

First, recognize the changes that are taking place in your life. This involves introspection which for many may be a limited skill. Many men are unaccustomed to looking inside themselves for any length of time.

This aversion to introspection, which some men feel, has come about from trained neglect. It limits them from sensitivity to themselves and others and creates barriers. It promotes confusion about what is happening to them at mid-life. Often those around the man notice him changing but if they point this out to him, he becomes defensive. Observations are regarded as criticisms and attacks rather than helpful suggestions.

The best response a man can make at this time is to be receptive to the comments of others and to his own inner reflections. Listen to others—their observations and suggestions; determine the common theme of what is being said. Asking God to drain defensiveness and give new insight into yourself can be an important item for your prayer life.

The second step is to acknowledge what these changes represent and why they are occurring. This is difficult because it is a step of admission. Then the question needs to be faced and answered: "Will I take action and if so what kind?"

Acknowledging the changes is sometimes an act of resignation rather than working toward a resolution of changes. A man simply resigns himself to what he perceives as inevitable. It is difficult enough to admit these changes to himself, but admitting it to other men is next to impossible. Some men tend to interpret admission of change and failure to achieve goals as a sign of weakness rather than an act of strength.

To ease the pain of admission there are several things a man can do: First, he can *become acquainted* with the mid-life crisis and its characteristics. There are some excellent books on the subject such as *The Forty to Sixty-Year Old Male* by Michael E. McGill; *Men in Mid-Life Crisis* by Jim Conway; and *Halfway up the Mountain* by David C. Morley. Learning about the mid-life crisis will help him realize that he is not alone. Through reading and observation he will come to realize that *he* controls the crisis and can determine whether the consequences will be positive or negative. Knowing that others have survived this experience will encourage him to move forward.

Second, he should *discuss his feelings* with others. This is the most effective step as contrasted with merely reading about the crisis. As he is able to share his feelings with another he will realize that such acknowledgement is actually painless. Once he gets his feelings out in the open he will realize that something must be done. He must take action. Ignoring the problem will no longer be possible. He must either live with the situation or act upon it.

Third, he must *consider the consequences.* A man needs to think of what response to this crisis would be best for him. If the response is REFLECTIVE, the progress can be more positive. Too often, though, the response is REFLEXIVE.

There are two basic forms of reflexive responses—passive acceptance and active affirmation.

Passive acceptance of the crisis is one of the easiest responses for many men because his new sense of self is under so much threat. He continues to live, changing neither his identity nor his behavior. He continues to suffer the effects of the crisis whether they be depression or erratic behavior. Because of his passivity he loses much of his excitement, vision and vitality for life. These men suffer and survive in silence.

Other men intensify their behavior in an attempt to actively *affirm* who they are. They try harder to do what they have been doing for so many years. This helps them thwart the immediate threat but it is merely an act of postponement. They are still vulnerable to crisis later on because they have not really altered the source of their identity. Many men choose this route because they can continue to do what they have always done with more effort and involvement.

The *reflective response* to the crisis is far more productive. The major difference between a reflexive response and a reflective response is a difference between resignation/relief and real resolution. After a man recognizes and acknowledges the crisis, his next step is to consider the consequences. He needs to refrain from responding with a reflexive response and consider change. Men who are most effective in handling the mid-life crisis are those who are able to build their sense of identity upon more than one source. They are able to develop a constructive, healthy identity as they expand their awareness of who they are. This is a wise step for they then discover new behaviors and a new meaning for their life. These new changes in behavior and how they see themselves involve a risk and they must be given careful consideration.

Most men who search for a new source of identity cannot discover this alone. He needs the assistance of others who know him well to help him identify other meanings for his life and identity. All too frequently a man is blind to alternative sources of meaning for his life. Others who are trusted can encourage, push and guide him to discover and analyze alternate sources of identity.

This step involves risk. A man must reach out and trust

another person in a close and caring relationship. This close-ness, however, may be just what he has been avoiding for many years. He needs to find someone with whom to share who will be committed to this closeness because he values the relationship. The other individual needs to be understanding, capable of keeping a confidence, and competent to deal with the issues of a mid-life crisis. Usually the person is one who has experienced intimate sharing in his/her own life, perhaps with the man who is struggling with the crisis. The relation-ship is already such that there are no barriers to their com-munication. The person can be approached with any concern or problem by the middle-aged man.

The middle-aged man needs to evaluate all of his relation-ships to discover such a person. It could be someone at work, a minister, sports companion, wife, etc. Hopefully, he will find one relationship which holds the promise of the above-men-tioned characteristics and begin to deal with the troublesome issues. It is best to limit this relationship to another male with the exception of his wife.

Fourth, he must *choose to change*. It is not easy, for many men see only the dark side of potential change.

One of the dilemmas of the male mid-life crisis is when the crisis was caused by events that were forced upon him, and can be resolved only by his making some changes. Although the initial circumstances were forced upon him, he can now take charge of the required changes. Ignoring them or wish-ing they had not occurred does not work. Nor does trying to prove to himself that he has not changed. What is needed is a time of reflection and careful consideration of the past and future changes. If a radical change is attempted immediately without considering the process and consequences, the chaos can continue.

Often a man will resist further change unless he feels that he can *choose* to change, not that he *has* to change. He must choose a way to change which involves others, rather than leaving them out. If other significant people around him, such as his family and close friends, see his changes as helping both him and his relationships, they in turn will support and encourage him. But resistance may further cripple him. Often friends and family may need to consider some of their own attitudes and insecurities which may be perpetuating his struggles.

An example of this is a man who feels he must change his job in order to resolve his own crisis. Family members may see this as a negative disruption of their life and resist his efforts. They may also resist his efforts to change social involvements, churches or hobbies. This is too threatening to them. Too many today opt for the security of sameness rather than risking change with the hope of growth. Instead of being encouraging and supportive, too often the response of those around him ranges from passive acceptance and tolerance to joking.

Even a man's desire to get into physical shape by working out, changing to a more casual wardrobe (such as wearing cowboy boots) can become the focal point for jokes and sarcasm.

In the past seven years I have experienced several transitions which Levinson discussed in *The Seasons of a Man's Life*. Each began with restlessness and dissatisfaction with what I was doing vocationally. The first occurred at age 37 when I realized that the interest of my life had shifted directions. I used to be interested in Christian education but my major focus had shifted to marriage and family ministries. Fortunately, I was able to remain in teaching but shift my subject area. This was satisfying for several years. But when I assumed directorship of a graduate department there was less time for students, teaching and counseling and more administrative work. In time I felt a bit frustrated and hemmed in but I tried to make adjustments. Eventually, the challenge of teaching and administration diminished and a new challenge surfaced as I developed and expanded a new counseling center. This new endeavor required a minimum amount of administrative time. Perhaps the other enticement involved being able to create, develop and work for myself without the procedures and limitations of a large organization. I had tried to think of how to eliminate some of the (to me) unchallenging administrative work. I thought of quitting. I thought of moving from full- to half-time teaching. What would it cost me? Could we afford it? It would mean cutting my regular salary in half and perhaps losing some of the benefits. I also considered how this would affect my wife, Joyce.

One evening I began sharing with Joyce my thoughts and feelings, what my desires and tentative plans were at that point in time. I wanted to teach just half time, spend the remainder in counseling, and also cut down some of my total involvement in work. I was experiencing some physical exhaustion and stress and knew it was time to cut back.

After sharing this with Joyce her response was, "Whatever you decide to do, I'll support you." That statement was the final affirmation I needed.

The fifth and final step is called the *integration of the change*. This occurs when a man brings together his new sense of self and new behaviors into a new pattern of life. These new behaviors will need reward and recognition from others no matter how small the recognition is.

How long will this process of resolution take? Weeks, months, or even years. And it will depend on the nature of the crisis itself, the man seeking a resolution and the response he receives from others.

The Christian Meaning of Mid-life

Hopefully the Christian can see a different meaning in the mid-life changes. For some, the changes are threatening. For a Christian they present an opportunity to apply his faith and develop further toward maturity. It is not a burn-out time of life, but a time of both harvest and new beginning, a time of enrichment and stability. Our interpretation of life and its events can change. The dismay and despair of confronting disappointments and unreached expectations can be shifted to realistic acceptance. As we learn from the past, the future can be different.

David C. Morley puts it this way:

To the Christian these middle-life changes have a different meaning. The change that is so threatening to the nonbeliever is an opportunity for the Christian to exercise his faith and to experience the process of true Christian maturity. The mature Christian is a person who can deal with change. He can accept all of the vicissitudes of life and not deny nor complain about them. He sees them all as the manifestation of God's love. If God loves me, then He is going to provide an experience that makes life richer and more in line with His will. To the Christian, "All things work together for good to them that love God . . ." (Romans 8:28). How often we hear that Scripture quoted. How little we see it applied to real-life experiences. What God is really saying is that we should comfort ourselves with the thought that what happens in our lives, victory or defeat, wealth or poverty, sickness or death, all are indications of God's love and His interest in the design of our lives. If He brings sickness to us, we should be joyful for the opportunity to turn to Him more completely. So often in the bloom of health, we forget to remember the God who has provided that health. When we are in a position of weakness, we are more likely to acknowledge His strength, we are more likely to ask His guidance every step of the way.[8]

With change and loss of youth may come a mourning experience. The painful feelings of our lost youth need to be discussed with a trusted and respected friend. The time of mourning can be a time of healing and new growth.

This is also a time to take responsibility for our lives and the situation in which we find ourselves. There is a tendency to blame others, circumstances and God. But each person for the most part creates his own traps. Therefore, we need to identify any snares we are using on ourselves and develop creative alternatives. This can be done by evaluating personal strengths and weaknesses, setting goals and selecting alternatives.

Here are some questions to ask yourself.
1. What areas of my life do I find satisfying?
2. What areas of my life do I find meaningless?
3. Am I living in accord with my values?
4. Am I working at something I believe in?
5. What would I like to work at?
6. Do I have any outside interests in addition to work?
7. When was the last time I tried something new?
8. Do I exercise my mind and my imagination?

Flexibility is essential. Those who are mentally healthy are able to adjust to changing circumstances to a greater degree. They are less compulsive and more relaxed and have found new sources of gratification when old ones are no longer available.

Being aware of the gamut of feelings and expressing them is important. If they are buried they control you. Discovering what creates positive and happy feelings is just as important as searching out the causes of anger or rage.

Evaluate what you can and cannot do at this time of life.

Evaluate what you can and cannot change about yourself. Ask, "What would be the result if I did this?" to several alternatives.

Discuss and evaluate new ideas with other trusted individuals. Start with small challenges, undertaken one step at a time.

How then should mid-life be viewed? What are the possibilities?

David Morley says,

[The] Christian should not fear the middle passage of his life. He should view this period as a time of enrichment. The flurry of youth is passed. His life begins to fall into step with reality. He sees that he can gain a measure of control. His tastes become more discriminating. He begins to enjoy the things that he has, rather than long for the things he cannot have. He begins to learn about patience and endurance. The need for immediate gratification has diminished because he has learned that sometime in life we have to wait and the time of waiting ought to provide knowledge that one could not get in any other way. He is not afraid to face the reality of his aches and pains. He faces the reality of their meaning and does something about it. He does not continue the unchecked appetites of youth. He modifies his appetites to meet his needs. He sees that the needs diminish as the metabolism slows down. He accepts that as a fact of life and takes the position of responsibility by doing something about it. He begins to enjoy the security of control that he has in all areas of life. No longer driven by every wind and doctrine and every impulse that comes his way, his course is straight and true, and the radiance of that life beams out to the world the message of inner peace. And that is worth more than volumes of words.[9]

Notes

1. M. Brown, "Keeping Marriage Alive Through the Middle Age," *McCall's*, January, 1973, pp. 73, 138-140.

2. Robert Lee and Marjorie Casebier, *The Spouse Gap* (Nashville: Abingdon Press, 1971), p. 128.

3. Richard P. Olson, *Mid-Life: A Time to Discover, a Time to Decide* (Valley Forge, PA: Judson Press, 1980), p. 62, as quoted in Laurence J. Peter, *Peter's Quotations* (New York: William Morrow and Company, Inc., 1977), p. 330.

4. Jim Conway, *Men in Mid-Life Crisis* (Elgin, IL: David C. Cook, 1978), pp. 17,18.

5. Daniel J. Levinson, *The Seasons of a Man's Life* (New York: Ballantine Books, 1978), pp. 198,199.

6. Michael E. McGill, Ph.D., *The Forty- to Sixty-Year-Old Male* (New York: Simon and Schuster, 1980), p. 69.

7. Ibid., pp. 224-247, adapted.

8. David C. Morley, *Halfway up the Mountain* (Old Tappan, NJ: Fleming H. Revell, 1979), p. 26.

9. Ibid., pp. 26,27.

Five

Preventing a Crisis

What can a man do to prepare for his future? Is there something he can do in the early years that will prevent a crisis from occurring later on? Yes, there is! The secret is to develop an immunity to the threats to your identity. We cannot do away with the threats themselves. No one's life is completely free from pressure, stress or threat. But there are some ways in which you can prepare yourself for the problems of later life. The most important is called "identity formation."

We need to examine who we are and what we are building our identity upon. Are we free to be different rather than conform to certain prescribed "male" roles? Often boys are channeled into specific areas and are taught to conform themselves to this endeavor and deny their true feelings and emotions. There is a machine mentality about such thinking, but it has been quite prevalent in this country. "Men *do* certain things and succeed in certain areas and men *do not* feel or express emotion." Consequently, men are often stifled from doing and becoming all God meant them to be.

The answer to the identity crisis is fourfold: (1) Build an adequate identity upon a solid base; (2) Become more complete in our humanity by experiencing and expressing feelings; (3) Develop strong friendships with other men; (4) Prepare for life crisis and changes by incorporating God's Word into our lives. We will explore each of these areas in detail.

Build an Adequate Identity

Our identity, our sense of who we are, is based upon who God is and how He views us.

When God said "Let Us make man in Our image" (Gen. 1:26, *NASB*), He once and for all provided a basis for human dignity, worth and value. He sealed forever the fact that every person who walked this earth would have the right to see himself as a creature of worth, value, and importance. This is another aspect of biblical self-love.

The main cause of a mid-life crisis is when a man's identity is threatened. The more a man centers his identity in just one phase of his life—such as vocation, family, or career—the more vulnerable he is to threats against his identity and the more prone he is to experience a crisis. A man who has limited sources of identity is potentially the most fragile.

Men (and women too) need to broaden their basis for identity. They need to see themselves in several roles rather than *just* a teacher, *just* a salesman, *just* a handsome, strong male, *just* a husband.

A man as early as possible needs to develop himself as a whole person. He must see himself as one with numerous talents, and varied interests and should discover his spiritual gifts. His sense of identity should have a broad base.

This necessitates being reliant not just upon himself but on others—and especially upon God. Instead of being defensive and closed he needs to be open to the opinions of others, especially of what they value in him. A Christian man does not stand alone for he is related to the other members of the Body of Christ. The potential of close fellowship and honest relations with others gives greater security. Looking into the Word of God to determine what it says about both God and man gives yet another source of identity. If a man has multiple sources for his identity he is less vulnerable to threats. A man has a choice of isolation or involvement.

This was described by Dr. Michael McGill:

The ships we have taught our boys to build are unfit to sail the seas they face as men. Their ships are sinking. The little island they scurry to only separates them from themselves. How much better it would be to teach our young men when they are boys and beyond that there is in every other person a part of who they themselves are. They can only come to know themselves as they invest themselves in relationships with those other people. To set for them an example wherein they see that their experience of themselves is limited only by their experience of others. If they choose to isolate themselves from personal relationships, to cut themselves off from others' perceptions of them, then they choose by that same process to limit themselves to a narrow identity, vulnerable to threats and ultimately to crisis. But if they choose to fully invest themselves in relationships with others, to draw from their experience with others a variety of perceptions of who they are as individuals and how they might behave in the world, then they open up to themselves the full range of potential identities and behaviors. A range of identities that is rich and rewarding, a range that really knows no limits, a range that forever provides them with an avenue for affirmation, a diverse sense of self from which they can withstand threats. Then only can they respond creatively and constructively to change and experience a full life from its beginning through the middle years to its end. A man in his middle years is not too old to discover this message. He is not too old to reach out to others and find in those others a new self. His ship may be sinking but his salvation is in swimming to others, not in seeking the inviting little island. He is too old and it is too late to go back on his life, but the time is just right for changing, for embracing new relationships, new ideas, discovering a new self and building a better second half.[1]

The bedrock for our self-esteem is the *fact* that we are created by the hand of God and in His image. Just as a book reflects its author, you and I reflect a portion of God's character. We are said to be His "likeness" (Gen. 1:26). Like God, we have great intellectual capacities. We are able to amass vast amounts of knowledge and use this information to make complex decisions. Like God, we also have the capacity for self-determination. We can plan ahead, foresee results, and make major choices that affect our destiny. We also have the capacity for language and we have great creative ability. We are able to explore nature, produce new inventions and create great works of art. We can use our genius for the service of mankind.

But the image of God goes deeper still. We have a moral nature that enables us to deal with spiritual and ethical matters. God built into Adam and Eve an inherent goodness. They were not morally neutral computers; their moral nature was stamped into the center of their being by the hand of God. We know that God was pleased with His creation because the book of Genesis states that He "saw all that He had made, and behold, it was very good" (Gen. 1:31, *NASB*).

Jesus Christ invites us to come to Him by faith, believing that He will accept us as we are into His family. "But as many as received Him, to them He gave the right to become children of God, even to those who believe in His name, who were born not of blood, nor of the will of the flesh, nor of the will of man, but of God" (John 1:12,13, *NASB*).

When we have the assurance that we are *special* because of God's unconditional love, we no longer need to constantly strive to create our own identity.

All of us want to feel competent, and worthwhile, and to belong. What is it like to belong? It is the awareness of being wanted, accepted, cared for, and enjoyed. Often we gain this through performance and achievements at work.

Worthiness is feeling that "I am good"; "I count"; "I am all right." People feel worthy when they do what they think they should. The feeling is confirmed when we sense that others have felt positively toward us. We look for their endorsement of our actions. A feeling of worthiness is related to a sense of being right and doing right in our eyes and in the eyes of others. It is important to determine who the people are whose response we are seeking. At work it is probably our employer or fellow employees. When do you feel most worthy? Who are the significant people from whom you desire acceptance?

Competence is a feeling of adequacy. It is feeling "I can"; "I have the ability or strength to do it." Our feeling of adequacy is built upon present as well as past accomplishments. It is based upon the achievement of goals and ideals we have set for ourselves. If I base it upon unrealistic standards or the feedback of others I will find instability. But if I base it upon what God has done for me, it is possible.

You and I have been accepted with an unconditional acceptance even though we are imperfect. "Therefore if any man is in Christ, he is a new creature; the old things passed away; behold, new things have come" (2 Cor. 5:17, *NASB*). We are God's new creation—we are His workmanship. The one who had the only perfect self-concept, Jesus Christ, is now our model. Our sense of being somebody comes through our relationship with Him. "Put on the new self who is being renewed to a true knowledge according to the image of the One who created him" (Col. 3:10, *NASB*).

Because of our position in Christ we know that we are accepted by God. We belong to Him. "He hath made us accepted in the beloved" (Eph. 1:6, *KJV*). Because God has forgiven us of our sins, we can say with conviction that we are good and worthwhile. "Therefore having been justified by faith, we have peace with God through our Lord Jesus Christ" (Rom. 5:1, *NASB*). And if God and Jesus Christ are with us at all times then we know we are not inferior or inadequate. We have a complete identity.

Dr. Lloyd Ahlem in *Do I Have to Be Me?* clearly summarizes what God has done for us:

> The writers of Scriptures are careful to point out that when God looks at you in Jesus Christ, He sees you as a brother to His own Son. Because of the work of Christ, all the ugliness of humanity is set aside. God has absolutely no attitude of condemnation toward man. You are worth all of God's attention. If you were the only person in the whole world, it would be worth God's effort to make Himself known to you and to love you, He gives you freely the status and adequacy of an heir to the universe.
>
> This is agape love, the unmerited, unconditional favor of God for man. We achieve our adequacy through

this unceasing love. We do not become sufficient, approved, or adequate; rather we are declared to be such! When we believe this, we become achievers and humanitarians as an effect, a by-product of our new-found selves.[2]

God's love fulfills our need for competence and identity!

Express Your Feelings

The second step in preventing a crisis is learning to feel emotions and to express them. Feelings and the expressions of those feelings are a relief valve for man. Becoming emotionally expressive is equivalent to becoming fully human. Since we have often been taught to shut up our emotions, perhaps we need a positive model of a total emotionally expressive man. Jesus experienced a wide range of emotions. His compassion and love were the most dominant. He frequently expressed emotions of sorrow and joy. On occasion He wept and sighed deeply in an expression of sorrow. Jesus spoke of you and expressed it (see Luke 10:21). He expressed anger and indignation on several occasions (see Mark 3:5; Matt. 23:27,33). He experienced deep grief, distress and even depression in His garden experience (see Matt. 26:37-41).

For many men, their emotions are almost totally repressed. As boys reared in our society they were taught not to show emotion. But such repression keeps us from expressing the entire gamut of our feelings. It is difficult to share a feeling you are out of touch with or have trouble identifying. Some men "feel" emotions but have a minimal understanding of what those emotions are. Thus any expression of emotion may be indirect. For example, there is a unique relationship between how a man builds his identity and how he views feelings.

The process of blending success into identity occurs early in life. A young boy soon learns to value himself and derive value from others through achievements, victories and successes. He is taught to never rest on his laurels but constantly move ahead. Winning, succeeding and being strong bring praise and rewards. He internalizes other significant attitudes until he learns to parent himself. He says nice rewarding things to himself when he achieves and derogatory comments when he fails.

The process can be described in this fashion:

His moods and emotions will become intertwined with his successes and failures. When he has won, proven himself, or performed well he'll feel elated. When he fails or disappoints he will feel depressed, ashamed, and embarrassed.

In time, however, he will learn to control and hide all of his feelings until his spontaneous or genuine responses are replaced by appropriately controlled ones. The ones that "work," make him seem strong and enable him to project the appropriate image.

At first these emotional controls will be erratic. Periodically, feelings will break through that he fears have spoiled his image as a "winner." Increasingly, however, these will get sorted out until the un-selfconscious moments become fewer and fewer while he becomes more and more polished. This process of becoming polished will feel so good to him that he won't even be aware of how he is totally losing touch with himself, giving up his true responses for the well-programmed ones designed to make him a better success machine.

Even his closest friendships with other boys will be contaminated by the fact that he's constantly being compared to them by others and he is constantly comparing himself to them. Being friends feels good but being better becomes even more important.

As he grows older, other boys are seen less as friends and more as competitors, potential threats to his own success pursuits. Therefore, he begins to become more guarded around them, hiding his weaknesses, inadequacies, and vulnerabilities. When his friends become too emotional, he becomes uncomfortable. He won't feel he can trust a friend who can't control his emotions.[3]

Some men do not even have a sufficient vocabulary to express their emotions. In learning to be men they learned to value expressions of masculinity and to devalue what they label "feminine" expressions.

Many men even seem to be locked up emotionally when they try to relate to each other. They are not comfortable sharing their failures, anxieties or disappointments. Their masculine image may be threatened if they appear to be weak or a complaining loser. Some are uncomfortable sharing successes or ecstasies for fear of appearing out of control or of inciting competitive jealousies.

Few men have experienced openness and vulnerability in their relationships. Thus they do not know what they are missing. Because of being socialized to repress and deny feelings in order to appear "masculine," their feelings are unknown and threatening to strangers.

Men have taken numerous positions concerning feelings. Some feel that all feelings are phoney. They are a waste of time and impractical. A cynical and bitter response protects them from their fear of feelings.

Others believe that all feelings are "weaknesses." To share them would give an indication that they are not as independent and capable as they seek to appear. Masculinity means not depending on anybody. They equate dependence with being a parasite and when they do have to depend upon someone they may feel distrustful and anxious. This has been the pattern of man throughout thousands of years as evidenced in Scripture. Man does not want to be dependent upon God either. He wants to do it himself and has difficulty trusting God.

Some men use their intellect to defend against feelings. They may dissect, analyze and discuss them but they do not spontaneously share them. They create distance between themselves and others through intellectualizing.

What is the role of a wife in helping her husband develop his emotionality? Her involvement can be very important. A wife can help her husband acknowledge that he has feelings inside of him. By learning to share feelings their own relationship will be enhanced. A wife might say to her husband: "I'm interested in knowing about the most interesting experience you had at work today (or this week)." "What are some of the emotions you've had this week and what caused them?" "I feel there's a portion of you I don't know about. If I had to describe how you feel about (name something), what would I say?" "You really seem to enjoy your woodworking. What is it that you enjoy so much about it?" "When you were a child, what were your greatest delights and your greatest fears?"

This means a wife must be supportive, encouraging and give positive reinforcement. The last response a man wants when he shares is any type of value judgment or put-down. A wife may be shocked or upset by his feelings, but "Can you tell me some more about that?" may be the safest reply. If a wife asks how he feels about his job and he says he hates it and wants to quit, she may feel threatened and respond with, "You can't! Think of us and your children!" Her husband probably will clam up from then on. A wife doesn't have to agree with her husband's feelings but her goal must be not to debate but to build communication and intimacy.

If a man wants to grow emotionally, he may, at times, feel uncomfortable. But the rewards are well worth the temporary discomfort.

Form Friendships with Men

A third step in preventing an identity crisis is forming close friendships with other men. Forming close relationships with other men takes change and courage. The Word of God encourages and admonishes us to develop close relationships because we *are* members of the Body of Christ. We are all to encourage, build up, help, bear one another's burdens. This cannot be accomplished when distance exists. Friendship is essential and biblically based.

Proverbs 17:17 (*AMP*): "A friend loves at all times, and is born, as is a brother, for adversity."

What are the characteristics of a friend? The book of Proverbs gives several guidelines. A friend is a person who is a man of peace. He is both reluctant to start strife or to spread it (see 3:29,30; 25:8,9). He is also kind and generous in his judgments (see 24:17,19).

He understands that silence is often wiser than criticism (see 11:13). He knows that when a person fails he need help rather than contempt.

He is a person of constancy. He is a friend who sticks closer than a brother and loves at all times (see 18:24 and 17:17). He is a man of candor as seen in Proverbs 27:6 and 29:5. He gives wise counsel both in the sense of good fellowship and sharing opposing viewpoints.

He has respect for the feelings of another. He avoids being jovial at the wrong time, being cruel, and carrying a joke too far.

If a man desires to develop some long-lasting, intimate friendships at any point in life, how can this be accomplished? There are some guidelines to follow which have helped many men move from sterile to fulfilled relationships.

1. *First of all, make a list of those attributes* which you respect in another man and those which you dislike. Do this by yourself.

The positive attributes should include personality characteristics that bring joy, the freedom to be yourself, a willingness to open up and reveal yourself as a person, a sense of trust and safety, a desire to be talkative, humorous and even silly, an eagerness to explore, expand and risk, and a receptiveness to learning new things when you are around that person.

Negative attributes would include characteristics that tend to make *you* feel pessimistic, distrustful, guarded, inhibited, uncreative, bored, depressed, resentful, and scared about life when you are in that person's presence. This kind of person restricts you by his very presence.

2. *Draw a circle with you in the center and the men that you consider potential friends in circles around you.* Place those you feel more distant from in circles which are progressively further away.

3. *Define in specific terms the characteristics you like and dislike about each of the persons indicated.* The following questions may be helpful:

(a) Does he remind me of someone from my past—friend or relative?

(b) Is he guarded and secretive around me and do I feel guarded and secretive around him? In other words, do I feel as if I'm prying whenever I ask him something personal? Do I have a feeling of regret when I tell him something intimate about myself? Does he volunteer personal information about himself freely when he's around me? Do I feel a strong desire to be open about myself when I'm around him? Is this a reciprocal relationship?

   (c) Do I feel comfortable going over to see him on the spur of the moment? Do I feel I have to plan each meeting with him carefully, well in advance, and only for a specific reason?

   (d) Do I feel comfortable calling him? Would he call me up for no other reason than to say hello?

   (e) Do I feel respected and appreciated when I'm around him? Do I sense that he has similar feelings toward me?

   (f) Do I have envious and competitive feelings toward him and do I sense that he has similar feelings toward me?

   (g) Does he say and do things that embarrass me and do I seem to make him uncomfortable?

   (h) Would I feel comfortable asking him to drive me to the airport, lend me his car, or give me a place to sleep if I needed it? Would I feel comfortable doing these things for him?

   (i) Do I feel I can grow and learn through a relationship with him? Do I feel that I can provide the same kind of atmosphere and opportunity for him? Again is this reciprocal?

   (j) Am I eager to know him as a total person or am I just interested in getting him to share a specific activity? Would I otherwise prefer not to get close to him?

   4. Once you have determined who is a potential friend, it is important to *recognize the importance of trust and dominance*. Is there going to be mutual trust? Is there going to be mutual give-and-take or will one dominate the other?

   To handle the issue of dominance, work toward sharing power and decision-making so that neither of you winds up in the shadow of the other.

   5. *Get together on a regular basis*, perhaps once a month, a time specifically set aside to keep your relationship up-to-date and to avoid hidden injustice collecting. ("I always call him but he never calls me.") Discuss any incident or remarks that were made by either of you which caused disappointment or discomfort. In other words, be open with each other regarding areas of abrasion before they create great rifts.[4]

Get into God's Word
The fourth step in building stability is to incorporate God's

Word into your life. This means taking portions of Scripture and dissecting them—asking what each says and what it means for your life. It means visualizing how you will put the passage into practice in specific situations. Consider these passages:

James 1:2,3 (Phillips): "When all kinds of trials and temptations crowd into your lives, my brothers, don't resent them as intruders, but welcome them as friends! Realize that they come to test your faith and to produce in you the quality of endurance. But let the process go on until that endurance is fully developed, and you will find you have become men of mature character with the right sort of independence."

Isaiah 41:10 (*AMP*): "Fear not: [there is nothing to fear] for I am with you; do not look around you in terror and be dismayed, for I am your God. I will strengthen and harden you [to difficulties]; yes, I will help you; yes, I will hold you up and retain you with My victorious right hand of rightness and justice."

Isaiah 43:2 (*AMP*): "When you pass through the waters I will be with you, and through the rivers they shall not overwhelm you; when you walk through the fire you shall not be burned or scorched, nor shall the flame kindle upon you."

Jeremiah 33:3 (*AMP*): "Call to Me and I will answer you and show you great and mighty things, fenced in and hidden, which you do not know—do not distinguish and recognize, have knowledge of and understand."

Asking for assistance in learning how to apply the Scripture is a positive move. Too frequently a man feels, "I can do it myself." Meeting regularly with other seeking men who desire a different life-style can lead to new insights and applications. Ask one of the respected and transparent men of your congregation for the opportunity to meet with him for discipling purposes. During this time learn how this man developed his relationship with his wife, his friends and God. Ask specific, pointed, personal and feeling-level questions.

Perhaps some of these suggestions sound foreign, awkward or uncomfortable to you. Although they sound simple they are really difficult, for they involve change and risk. Fear of change often cripples us from growth.

Jesus came to release us from the imprisonment of sameness. You and I are love objects—God's love objects. God says, "I love you." It is not a love based on our love either first or after His response. Because of His love we can love Him and others. He is asking us to relate to others through His strength. If you try it, your life will be different.

Notes
1. Michael E. McGill, *The Forty- to Sixty-Year-Old Male* (New York: Simon and Schuster, 1980), pp. 277,286,287.
2. Lloyd H. Ahlem, *Do I Have to Be Me?* (Ventura, CA: Regal Books, 1973), p. 64.
3. Herb Goldberg, *The Hazards of Being Male* (New York: A Signet Book, 1976), pp. 115,116.
4. Ibid., pp. 138-140, adapted.

Six

The Season of the Empty Nest

The family is dispersed. There are empty bedrooms in the house and the parents no longer have to retreat to their own bedroom for privacy. The two-seat car has replaced the station wagon. The children are independent and have their own relationships and life goals. They are gone.

Do we resist or regret their leaving? Do we encourage it like eagles do with their offspring? When an eagle is born he is not very attractive. He looks like he is all neck with a head and body attached. His parents feed him often to the point of gorging, thus assuring his survival. He grows and develops until he is almost as large as his parents. Then he is ready for flying school. The parents know that in order to survive he must learn to fly.

If you were there you would be able to see the tension building between parents and eaglet. The mother will urge, coax and push her child to the edge of the nest. The eaglet resists with all the strength of its muscles, its talons dig into the nest. But the mother eagle continues pushing and finally shoves her child from the nest. If you were the eaglet's parent you would probably feel like yelling instructions to the plummeting eaglet. The bird continues to fall and seems uncoordinated in its efforts to right itself. Did its parent make a mistake? In time the eaglet spreads its wings and catches a draft. It discovers that it can sail safely to the ground. Then it learns to flap its wings as well as spread them. It learns more about wind timing and soon begins to hunt on its own. Soon the eaglet is able to leave the nest for good and becomes self-sufficient. Its parents knew how and when to release him.

There is a time for children to enter and a time for them to leave. There is a time for them to be dependent and a time to be independent. Like the eaglet there is a time when they must be free, physically and emotionally. God wants our children to become independent and free. He asks parents to cooperate with Him in that task.

For some couples the empty nest is a major crisis. Their sense of loss and change is very real. It is a mingling of numerous feelings as expressed in Ecclesiastes 3:1-8—a time of weeping, laughing, mourning, healing, loving, releasing, losing and embracing. The atmosphere of the home changes. There are fewer choices to make, less confusion and noise. Old habit patterns of shopping, cooking, scheduling—use of time—will change. New roles will have to be established and new pressures may occur. Needs formerly filled by children will be diverted to someone else for fulfillment. These needs include communication, affection and companionship. If couples rush toward each other demanding the other person to replace their previous interaction with a child, they may instead push their partner away.

Frequently the upheaval of children preparing to leave home hits at the same time as the mid-life crisis. Children affect a marriage not only when they arrive, but also when they leave.

Adjusting to the Leaving

Many studies show that when the last child grows up and leaves home there is an increased likelihood of marital maladjustment. This event acts as a marital catalyst, demanding that the husband and wife face themselves, each other, and their marriage in a new way. The longer they avoid this task, the faster the gap between them widens.

For one thing, the couple must make adjustments in their parental and spousal roles. This can be especially true for the mother who has devoted herself almost entirely to her children. When they leave she feels abandoned, unloved and uncared for. When her children grow up, the mother literally joins the ranks of the unemployed. She may begin to feel that there is little reason or justification for her life, that she has little to contribute to the process of living. She may experience "post-parental depression" and share the feeling of the mother who said she "felt like dying" when her last daughter got married.[1]

According to Gerald Klerman, M.D., of the Harvard Medical School, the departure of grown children often necessitates a major renegotiation of the marriage relationship. Suddenly a man and wife are thrown together with no one else to talk to. Though the "empty nest" syndrome is described as a maternal problem, the father often suffers a great deal when the last teenager cleans out his closet and takes down his posters. The child who was Mommy's little girl at six has become Daddy's special pal; and when she goes, he is devastated.[2]

So the experience of the empty nest is always something of a crisis. It can leave a devastating sense of emptiness and purposelessness. Loneliness can set in. The silent house is full of memories. There was once so much to do, and now there is so little. The crowded, busy years seemed arduous at the time. But now, looking back, it is clear that this was far outweighed by the deep, solid satisfaction of being needed.[3]

The groundwork for this traumatic experience for women is embedded in the conventional notion that in a good marriage the woman lives only for the collective values of being a wife and mother, with emphasis on the latter task since most of the care for the children falls on her shoulders. If she worked before marriage, she usually was expected to put all that behind her upon entering the wedded state. Even if she continued to work after marrying, she was expected to do so without neglecting her family duties. With such an expectation, it is no wonder that the woman, particularly the one who has devoted her life exclusively to motherhood, should undergo a terrific psychological change when all her children are gone. Rooms that once rocked with laughter and louder music now scream out in silence! If there has been little intimacy and companionship with her husband, the emptiness is even greater.

The father must also readjust to the empty nest, of course; but his job and other outside interests usually occupy his attention. Since he has not been as directly and constantly related to the children, his adjustment is less radical. Indeed, he may even breathe a sigh of relief when the children are finally out on their own. As they grew up, the mother's actual work load got somewhat lighter, but he felt increasing pressures for bigger allowances, more clothes, money for college, money to get started with a career or new home.[4]

Some men can become just as depressed if they are strongly involved in their role as a father. The involvement of a father with his children stems from various motivations. Some use it to demonstrate their concern, to express their own need for love and caring or as a means to structure their time and activity. Some men find more of their identity in being a father. Some find it equally as father and worker and when the father role ceases the worker role increases.

Men vary in their responses to the empty nest. Some attempt to hang onto the father role which their children may accept or reject. Others seek out other youth who allow them to function as a father. They may become involved in scouting or other youth groups where they can have an influence. Others react aggressively in anger and reject all young people and their behavior. Some in their anger and hurt find it easier to just avoid their own children and other youth. Others eagerly seek their new role and relish their newfound freedom.

When all the children leave home and the nest is empty, some parents have no idea who they are or what to do with themselves. Their identity, both as individuals and as family members, has been so tied up in mothering and fathering that they are lost. They feel worthless and useless. They feel robbed of their roles and of their children. The pain of separation, particularly from their own families of origin, is recalled. Although they mourn their loss, their children will be all right; they have everything to look forward to. The parents are not sure that they have anything to look forward to.

What do parents say to themselves as children leave? Listen to their thoughts. Will you think this or have you already had some of these thoughts?

"I miss the early years with my children. I was so tied up in work at that time."

"The nest doesn't seem to empty as fast as I want. They're sure slow in moving out."

"I looked at that small chair and started to cry. It seemed like yesterday my son was sitting in it."

"I'm sure I'll be glad when they will leave. But won't I feel useless?"

"That room seemed so empty when he left."

"I'm looking forward to a new job! This time for pay!"

"Now that they're gone, we sit, we don't talk, don't look at each other. Nothing!"

"Parenting is hard work and I want to get out of this job."

"We married at 20 and had the first one at 22. The last one came at 34. He left when he turned 21. Why didn't someone tell us it would take 29 years until we were alone again as a couple!"

"We're adjusted to their being gone. I hope none of them divorce or lose a job and have to move back. I like this setup!"

"I don't want to build my happiness on when they call, write or visit. I need my own life now."

"They left too soon, married too young and had kids too soon. I hope they realize I'm not their baby-sitter. I raised one family but I'm not going to raise another!"

"I've done what I could. They're in the Lord's hands now. And I guess they always have been, come to think of it."

On the other hand, parents, and mothers in particular, do know that children grow up and leave home. Empty-nest theoreticians do not give parents credit for foresight. Watching children grow up and away is an inherent aspect of rearing a family, although that does not negate the fact of loss and the very real depression families may experience over separation. But these feelings are not necessarily unexpected or devastating. In fact, some parents have very positive feelings about launching their children. It frees them to pursue other interests, to deepen relationships with other people, especially spouses, and perhaps to have different and more successful relationships with their adult children.[5]

Launching Your Child into the World

The developmental tasks of child-launching are twofold. If a child is going to college or into marriage he must be sent away with ceremony and proper equipment. For college this means a period of shopping for clothes, luggage and writing equipment. For marriage it means the hope chest, showers and wedding preparations. In either case it is interesting that in the United States, where the rites of passage into adolescence are often minimal, there are rituals that attend child launching. (When children leave home to take a job, there are usually very few rituals.) These events have the manifest function of simply preparing the one who is leaving for his or her future. But they have a more hidden function in helping the ones staying home over a difficult transition.

The transition begins when mother and father put the last boy on the airplane for a distant school or stand on the church steps and wave a final good-bye to their radiant youngest daughter. Their next days of behavior are veiled to their friends, but often both parents wander about the home looking at mementoes from an exhilarating past. They try to remember how these rooms, now so still, used to echo with rock and roll, loud laughter, or singing. Although they are somewhat comforted to know that their newly marrieds have promised to visit and that their college son will be back for vacation, they are aware that they won't ever really be home again. The daily tasks taken for granted all these years are suddenly laid aside. The responsibilities, often worrisome, are now relayed to others' shoulders; and the constant dynamo of adolescent activity is abruptly stilled.[6]

How do you handle the leaving of the last child when you feel you have been a failure as a parent? When your parenting seems incomplete and conflicts still exist? There are usually feelings of both pain and relief. A mother of five shared her feelings:

"It hurts that he's gone because things are terrible

between us now, and he doesn't come around much any more. But, I don't know, I think it's better since he's gone. It's a relief not to have to see him every day. Oh, I don't know. What can I say? It hurts not to see him, but it hurts more to see him and be reminded." (Forty-four-year-old typist, mother of five, married twenty-five years to a maintenance man.)

Yes, she's relieved that he's gone—glad not to be burdened by his presence, not to be reminded daily of her pain. But it hurts, too—hurts, because, even though he's not there, she can't help remembering, can't help believing she failed, can't help reflecting on the past with regret, can't help wondering how it could have been otherwise.

And there's something else as well. For those memories, those questions, mean also that the separation from the child is more difficult than usual because she's stuck with feelings of incompletion—with the sense that one of life's tasks is not finished, yet is now outside her control. It's somewhat akin to having to deal with the death of a parent with whom conflicts remain unresolved. The departing child is not dead, of course. But the psychological experience of the loss can be the same. Psychologically, it feels like it's the last chance to heal the divisions, the last chance to make peace. Thus, just as in a death, the departure of a child with whom there is conflict means that the loss is experienced more keenly, the grief more difficult to manage and work through.[7]

As parents we are expected at some point to relinquish our children. If this is done over a period of several years the process is much easier. Lack of forethought about the departure, along with an abrupt transition, can be traumatic.

Parents need to expect and accept changing relationships with their children. A parent does not remain forever in the authority position as with infants or preschoolers. Nor does the parent remain in the child-adult transition stage where the parent guides the child through questions rather than commands.

Releasing the Child

The last stage is release or relinquishment which is not easy but is necessary. This stage elevates the child to the adult-adult stage. As an adult, therefore, he/she is not given unsolicited advice. He is given the right to make his own decisions and to make mistakes. (Hopefully, he/she has had these same opportunities during adolescence.)

John White, a Christian psychiatrist, gives his description of releasing your child.

> In days gone by market men in Covent Garden, London, used to sell caged nightingales. They captured the birds and blinded them by inserting hot needles into their eyes. Because nightingales sing in the dark, a liquid song bubbled almost endlessly from the caged and blinded birds. Man had enslaved and blinded them to gratify his delight in their music. More than this he had enslaved them in such a manner that they could never again enjoy freedom. No one could set them free.

> To relinquish our children is to set them free. The earlier we relinquish them the better. If we unthinkingly view them as objects designed for our pleasure, we may destroy their capacity for freedom just as the Covent Garden men made nightingales "unfreeable." We may also cripple ourselves. Having made our children necessary to our happiness, we can so depend on them that we grow incapable of managing without them.

> Yet what is relinquishment? Clearly it must not mean avoiding our parental responsibilities. Our children need food, shelter, clothing, love and training, and it is our business to give them these. Nor does relinquishment mean to fail to teach our children respect and gratitude. Moreover, if we have the responsibility of their upbringing, we must have the authority to do whatever is necessary to fulfill that responsibility.

> To understand what relinquishment is we must first understand what God is like and what the essence of his relationship to us is. As he is to us, so must we (so far as possible) be to our children.

> God's attitude as a parent . . . combines loving care

and instruction with a refusal to force our obedience. He longs to bless us, yet he will not cram blessings down our throats. Our sins and rebellions cause him grief, and in his grief he will do much to draw us back to himself. Yet if we persist in our wrongdoing he will let us find by the pain of bitter experience that it would have been better to obey him.

To relinquish your children does not mean to abandon them, however, but to give them back to God and in so doing to take your own hands off them. It means neither to neglect your responsibilities toward them nor to relinquish the authority you need to fulfill those responsibilities. It means to release those controls that arise from needless fears or from selfish ambitions.[8]

Joyce Landorf describes relinquishing our children in this way:

Having children is a little like building ships. There comes a day when you have completed everything, and the ship needs to be launched. You christen it and send it gliding down to the sea of life. You trust it will not only float but sail! With your children, it's now up to God, and you trust Him even though you know all about the storms that may overtake them.[9]

What helps bridge the gap and fill the void of companionship? The most profound needs of companionship are tenderness and emotional support. We have already indicated that when the wife loses her role as mother, she has no one to turn to but her husband. A wife's great need for emotional support is one of the crises of her middle years. It is important for us to note this as we discuss role change in middle age. Traditionally it has been assumed that an American wife has few emotional resources outside her immediate home.[10] Yet in today's society she has many other resources to draw upon. A woman today has numerous options open to her. Her life can be seen as having three parallels. Here is one way for a woman to view her life.

My Interests   *My Marriage*   *My Children*

A woman needs to keep all three aspects moving and growing.

If she focuses on any one to the exclusion of the other, she will be in big trouble later on. Women have greater opportunities today to pursue all three aspects.

Preparing Ourselves for the Empty Nest

Perhaps there is too much focus upon what a couple is losing when their children leave. Let's talk now about what can be done to prepare for their departure and what the benefits are when the children leave home.

It is possible for couples to survive the empty nest and mid-life years and have a strong, fulfilling marriage.

The language used to describe this time period almost always conveys a negative impression. "The empty nest" conveys a feeling of sadness, uselessness, or "my function is over." Why not use words like "the awakening stage," "the freedom stage," "the growth stage," "the second honeymoon stage," or "the emergence"? This is a time of gain as well as loss. The empty nest does not have to be a crisis but simply a passageway between two eras in the life of the parents.

Many women (and men too) eagerly look forward to this time of life, and when it occurs they breathe a sigh of relief. They want the new freedom. These are parents who have planned for their children's release and whose identity is not tied up in their children. They have a life of their own separate from their children.

Some parents dream of the day in the future when they can return to the carefree, daring and impulsive persons they used to be—sleep late in the morning, make love in the family room, go out to dinner or take off for the weekend on five-minutes notice. In other words, they look forward to complete freedom.

This is a time of ending, but also a time of beginning. There is the potential for new experiences and adventure, but also the risk of failure. It is a time when fantasies of travel, more time for personal interests, a new career, more personal growth, a deeper marital relationship can come true. Yes, there is a bit of sadness as memories arise but above all it can be a time of celebration, awakening, rejoicing and change.

There are many rituals which still bind some parents and

children. These rituals can, in a sense, become a replacement for the children's presence in the home. They include regular dinners, vacation visits, phone calls, writing each week, celebration of special times like holidays, birthdays, etc. The children need as much say-so in these activities as the parents.

The empty nest is actually a progressive experience rather than an abrupt departure. But we don't usually realize it. I now see that this happened in my own life. My daughter and I were quite close as she was growing up. Somewhere during high school and the two years following we began to spend less and less time together. She felt more inclined toward her own activities and friends. She declined offers to go out to dinner with us or what seemed to us an exciting social event. The last year she was home it seemed as though we had a boarder rather than a daughter. She was there to sleep and perhaps eat but that was it. Then finally she took an apartment with a girl friend and the transition was complete. This pattern is quite normal and quite healthy. Consider the parents and child where the physical transition also includes all social and emotional contacts as well! The abruptness and intensity can be very stressful.

How do couples handle the change in a positive manner? Some couples experience a second honeymoon. Not the experience of Jean and John.

John came home just four months after their last daughter had gone off to college and found Jean crying; Jean had had high hope for the time when their children were gone. She had always wanted to write and had set off for a junior college in her area and enrolled in a writing class. She had many friends her age that she liked, and she was determined to renew relationships with them. She bravely told John that she was going to take golf lessons so that one day a week she hoped to play golf with him. None of this had materialized very well. Her English teacher was not enthusiastic about her short stories; her friends had their own lives and their own problems; her golf drives curled out into the rough. She recognized that all of these plans were not very substantial anyway. She had too much time alone and there was no sound in the house. But beyond that there was a void in her emotional life which neither writing, nor friends, nor golf would fill. She became more and more depressed, and finally could not conceal it from her husband.

When John heard her sobbing in their bedroom he climbed up the steps two at a time, took her in his arms, and comforted her. Then he patiently asked her to tell him what was wrong. As the story of her failure to adjust came out, he was patient and understanding. The next day he called his office and said he would not be in to work that day. It was springtime, and although he lived in a semi-desert area in California, he knew where the spring creeks were swollen and flowers blooming. He drove Jean there and they walked by the creek and recalled how the flowers had been in the Midwest in the springtime. That weekend he cancelled his golf game with his regular foursome and, instead, took Jean to a driving range and helped her with her bad drive. Afterwards they went out to a restaurant and danced. On Sunday they stayed home, had a late breakfast together, and spent the day talking-and-planning for the years to come. Jean's depression was gone.

Her depression was gone, but something else took its place. When John stayed home and then gave her his weekend, it was not the time with him alone that was important. It was his understanding of her feelings that buoyed her up. It was his attitude that neither his work nor his friends were as important to him as she that gave her the answer she needed. So of course she responded with deeper tenderness, and John was struck by what he had missed during the preceding years in their growing alienation. Together they planned each month to include more and more things both had secretly wanted to do but which had not been possible when the children were around.[11]

As you consider the experience of this couple there are five important elements in their adjustment:

1. They were able to develop a new kind of intimacy with each other as they moved from silence to words. John began

to call Jean every day from work. Their love was demonstrated through words and behavior.

2. They developed a new way of performing their roles. They experimented with household tasks and learned how to play, plan and work together.

3. They expanded their range of friendships, finding other couples who were in the same situation as they. Thus they were able to direct some of the emotional investment once spent on their children to these other couples.

4. They learned to develop a new role with their children. The parent-child role became an adult-adult relationship. They did not interfere in their children's lives nor did they push advice at them. They learned to be companions. This was made easier for Jean because John was fulfilling her emotional needs.

5. They also learned to give of themselves in service to others. This is a healthy way to direct emotional energy, and for us who know Jesus Christ it is one of our callings in life.

The following suggestions have been proven effective in helping couples prepare for the empty nest:

1. Establish priorities, with marriage at the top, early in your marriage. Some people are fearful that by doing this their careers or chances of success will suffer, but this has proved not to be the case. A lasting marriage takes commitment.

2. The demand of parenthood needs to be balanced with the needs and concerns of marriage. Daily, uninterrupted, open, intimate interaction between husband and wife must be planned. It does not just happen. This time together should be considered almost sacred.

3. Any signs of the relationship deteriorating such as jealousy, nagging, sarcasm, communication breakdown, etc. should be tended to immediately. Ignoring symptoms leads to indifference.

4. Encourage each other to develop your own spiritual giftedness. Individual potential needs to be cultivated and nurtured. Marriage is a relationship of equality. A lopsided, dominating relationship limits intimacy and growth.

5. A balance between individual development and growth and couple growth and development is essential. Companion-

ship is an adhesive which brings stability, not a suffocation togetherness.

6. Maintaining a strong and creative sexual relationship enhances concern for each other.

7. A support group is especially helpful. Developing helpful and interesting friendships with other couples can add stability to a relationship.

8. Complete a marital check-up periodically. This procedure can be done either by the couple themselves or with a third party who is skilled in helping couples. Marriage Enrichment retreats, classes, written materials can be used for this process. It is often risky but rewarding to attempt even positive changes. One may want to change and grow and the other may resist. A relationship needs the desire of both for rejuvenation.

9. Evaluate your job to avoid being locked into meaningless and frustrating work. Dissatisfaction with work has been identified as one of the major factors of the male mid-life crisis.

10. Alter your life-style from time to time to bring new life into your relationship. A life-style at one point in time may not be fulfilling later on.

11. If your spouse wants to leave you or become involved with someone else, do not give up. Problems need to be waited out patiently. Complete forgiveness is necessary for the marriage to survive.

What are some of the possible benefits of this mid-life time and the empty nest?

There can be fewer financial pressures, more freedom for recreation and travel, more time to build and enhance the marriage, freedom to make some major changes without affecting the children, greater maturity to evaluate your life and its direction.

The prospect of change and growth is threatening to some. Yet we do not face it alone, nor in our own strength. We are not limited by the past.

Christ's strength is all we need: "My grace is sufficient for thee: for my strength is made perfect in weakness" (2 Cor. 12:9, *KJV*).

Our past failures are blotted out: "No matter how deep the

stain of your sins, I can take it out and make you as clean as freshly fallen snow. Even if you are stained as red as crimson, I can make you white as wool!" (Isa. 1:18, *TLB*).

Christ has made us new people: "If any man be in Christ, he is a new creature: old things are passed away; behold, all things are become new" (2 Cor. 5:17, *KJV*).

We have nothing to fear: "He shall give his angels charge over thee, to keep thee in all thy ways" (Ps. 91:1, *KJV*). "Then make me truly happy by loving each other and agreeing wholeheartedly with each other, working together with one heart and mind and purpose" (Phil. 2:2, *TLB*). "May God who gives patience, steadiness and encouragement help you to live in complete harmony with each other—each with the attitude of Christ toward the other" (Rom. 15:5, *TLB*).

The best is yet to come!

Notes

1. Robert Lee and Marjorie Casebier, *The Spouse Gap* (Nashville: Abingdon Press, 1971), p. 132.

2. Ibid.

3. James A. Peterson, *Married Love in the Middle Years* (Chicago: Association Press, 1968), pp. 52,53.

4. Ibid., p. 59.

5. Mel Roman and Patricia E. Raley, *The Indelible Family* (New York: Rawson, Wade Publishers, Inc., 1980), pp. 205,206.

6. Peterson, *Married Love*, pp. 41,42.

7. Lillian B. Rubin, *Women of a Certain Age* (New York: Harper and Row Publishers, 1979), pp. 22,23.

8. John White, *Parents in Pain* (Downers Grove, IL: InterVarsity Press, 1979), pp. 164,165.

9. Joyce Landorf, *Change Points* (Old Tappan, NJ: Fleming H. Revell, 1981), p. 156.

10. Peterson, *Married Love*, p. 53.

11. Ibid., pp. 54,55.

Seven

The Open Season: Affairs and Unfaithfulness

So far we have talked about specific problems you may encounter at a particular stage in your life/marriage. But this chapter is about a problem that has no season—it's always a potential.

Fidelity is a calling which includes all who marry; and this calling is to extend through all ages of a marriage. We are admonished to forsake all others and cleave to our husband or wife, but we must remember that fidelity is more than just restraining a sexual drive toward someone other than our partner.

When couples marry they are called to be faithful, but to what? To sexual faithfulness alone or is there more? We are called to faithfulness in all areas of our life: to marriage itself as a calling; to the friendship phase of the marital relationship so that each comes to see the other as his best friend; to our partner as a child of God, a joint heir with us. And we are admonished to treat each other as such. Part of our calling in life is to minister to others in the name of Jesus Christ, and this means our partner as well.

Remember the phrase in the old wedding ceremony which

says "I plight thee my troth"? The word *troth* is an old English term which carries with it the pledge to be true, faithful, loyal and honest. It also involves trust, reliability and integrity. *Troth* carries with it the possibility of mutual intimacy, deep communication, the ability to trust and depend upon each other. To "plight thee my troth" means that I will actively work to include all of these characteristics in my marital relationship. Some people, however, are "faithful" to their partners but for a different reason.

Negative Fidelity
Lewis Smedes describes negative fidelity:

A man or woman can be just too busy, too tired, too timid, too prudent, or too hemmed in with fear to be seriously tempted by an adulterous affair. But this same person can be a bore at home, callous to the delicate needs of his partner. He or she may be too prudish to be an adventuresome lover, but too cowardly to be in honest communication and too busy to put himself out for anything more than a routine ritual of personal commitment. He/she may be able to claim that he/she never cheated; but he/she may never have tried to grow along with his/her partner into a deep, personal relationship of respect and regard within marriage. His/her brand of negative fidelity may be an excuse for letting the marriage fall by neglect into dreary conformity to habit and, with that, into dull routine of depersonalized sex. I am not minimizing the importance of negative fidelity; but anyone who thinks that morality in marriage is fulfilled by avoiding an affair with a third party has short-circuited the personal dynamics of fidelity."[1]

Unfortunately the thinking of most of us toward marital unfaithfulness is limited to sexual involvement. In a broader sense a large portion of couples have been unfaithful through involvement with some things rather than some one other than their spouse. When our thoughts are preoccupied with any divergence and our energies drained and sapped so that even leftovers are few and marriage is neglected, we are involved in an affair.

Men and women have affairs with their jobs, their hobbies, their TV, their children, their church. When some other event or activity or person takes precedence over our spouse and interferes with the development and growth of our marriage, a nonsexual affair is in effect.

Fidelity in marriage means that we are to protect it against any outside interference. Fidelity is positive and is based upon God's fidelity and vow to His people. God's fidelity to Israel was a faithful commitment regardless of their attraction and dalliances with others. He said: "And I will betroth you to Me forever; yes, I will betroth you to Me in righteousness and in justice, in lovingkindness and in compassion, and I will betroth you to me in faithfulness" (Hos. 2:19,20, *NASB*). God's fidelity was a commitment for the good of His people and their development and was meant to be a blessing. Fidelity means more than just avoiding affairs; it is a positive moving ahead with the development of a growing marriage.

I don't know of many who enter marriage with the plan, "I'm going to have an affair." The majority of people in our nation disapprove of extramarital affairs. Yet research indicates that at least one half of those married will have at least one affair. And it is totally naive to believe that it is just the non-Christians who become involved. Almost all the couples I know or have seen in counseling who have been involved in affairs are Christians. They seem to have one unique characteristic, however. I believe they delay going for help longer than non-Christians; also they are more secretive about their affairs.

Fidelity and Faithfulness

What were your vows to each other when you married? What was your expression of faithfulness and to what was it directed? Do you even remember your vows at this point in your life?

Marital vows today seem to have less meaning and commitment to the marrying couple than a generation ago. A vow is supposed to be binding regardless of personal need fulfillment, lack of love, the attraction of another, or incapacitating illness. Couples need to commit to a fidelity without any qualifications, limitations, or restrictions. For some, making a serious marital vow is difficult for they have little experience in being faithful to anything or anyone and are not aware of the high cost. Without the promise of fidelity, there can be no trust.

Faithfulness to a vow with no faithfulness to the growth and development of the marriage leads to emptiness, frustration and a feeling of being trapped.

For couples who built their marriage upon the trust of erotic love, with little thought or attention given to *agape* or *phileo* love, the struggle toward fidelity is greater. *Eros* is not the love which loves "in spite of." Agape, Christ's unconditional love, is our stabilizer. Eros is a fluctuating love based upon the fulfillment of a personal need. Eros is a passionate love that desires another person for self-gratification. It must be self-satisfying and is directed toward the person that can meet those needs. The slightest strain on a marriage can hinder the fulfillment of eros. Eros love cannot stand alone; it needs to be redeemed and attached to *agape* and *phileo* love to achieve balance. Agape love can enrich sexual love by seeing the other as a person worthy of respect and concern, rather than one who simply fulfills my needs. Agape brings in realism so we can see our partner as imperfect, accept him as such and realize our own lack of realistic expectations.[2]

What is adultery? Many people do not like the sound of that word. There is a harshness to it, a sense of violation and disloyalty which offends the ear. Adultery is the same in any culture—sexual intercourse with another person other than one's spouse.

The biblical account of an affair of which most of us are aware is that of David and Bathsheba. David in mid-life was involved with the complexities of leading his nation. Perhaps because of the numerous changes in his life and the stress and pressure he was under he was emotionally ready for an affair. In 2 Samuel 11:2-3 and 12:13-15 we read the account:

> Now when evening came David arose from his bed and walked around on the roof of the king's house, and from the roof he saw a woman bathing; and the woman was very beautiful in appearance.
>
> So David sent and inquired about the woman. And one said, "Is this not Bathsheba, the daughter of

Eliam, the wife of Uriah the Hittite?" (11:2,3 *NASB*).

Then David sent for her and when she came he slept with her. (She had just completed the purification rites after menstruation.) Then she returned home. When she found that he had gotten her pregnant she sent a message to inform him (vv. 4,5, *TLB*).

Then David said to Nathan, "I have sinned against the Lord." And Nathan said to David, "The Lord also has taken away your sin; you shall not die. However, because by this deed you have given occasion to the enemies of the Lord to blaspheme, the child also that is born to you shall surely die."

So Nathan went to his house (12:13-15, *NASB*).

In this account we see the common ingredient which is characteristic of adultery—it hurts. It violates fidelity. It violates troth.

James Olthius describes the purpose of the commandment concerning adultery.

"You shall not commit adultery" is an Old Testament way of restating the Word for marriage. It is not a prohibition aimed at holding down man's evil sexual lusts, but a positive protection for full troth fulfillment. The seventh commandment or Word simply tells man that only in troth and fidelity can marriage be a blessing. Today it should perhaps read: "Keep the troth in marriage," or even, "Have fun in marriage." The Scriptures warn man against adultery because it breaks troth, destroys mutual freedom, and makes people unhappy. The Word is a cryptic warning protecting marriage. Since marriage does not break as fast as a crystal glass, people flirt with the idea that fidelity is not really affected by an indiscretion here and there. However, the Word reminds us to take care. The commandment is much like the "No Swimming" sign planted in front of a dangerous pond. The signs go up because someone cares enough about life to try to prevent drowning. So it is with the seventh Word.

When God forbids adultery, he calls man to more than physical fidelity. Marriage is a total troth communion, which can be broken by any kind of infidelity, not

just physical, as we have traditionally too often assumed.[3]

A question commonly asked in counseling sessions is,
"Why did it have to happen?" What was the reason for this violation? Are there any common causes? And if there are, can
knowing about them help forestall any of us from such
involvement? Perhaps—

Why People Have Affairs

Why do people, many of whom have either a strong Christian conviction against adultery or a high sense of morality,
have affairs?

During mid-life, affairs are common occurrences. A man's
desire to recapture his fleeting youth and masculinity, coup-
led with a sense of stagnation in his own marriage, helps to
set the stage of infidelity. The same reasons can propel a
woman to another man. An affair can be used to cover up a
person's feelings of discontent. Dwight Small describes the
process:

The affair may be a welcome diversion, a momen-
tary tranquilizing of a burdensome, anxious situation
either in his career or at home. Here's a nice break
from hard reality. After all the tough years of keeping
his nose to the grindstone—and for what?—isn't it
time for a little reward in terms of romantic affirmation? Subconsciously, too, it may be the rather compelling need of the middle years to prove one's attractiveness at a time when confirmation from other quarters
has largely dried up. Soon it will be too late; it is now or
never!

What comes into such a man's life as a fresh, new
event is bound to be stimulating, especially when it is
secretive and furtive, risky enough to confirm his bold-
ness and daring. There is a curious new freedom he's
experiencing, perfectly understandable inasmuch as
there is no past as yet to regret, no future as yet to
dread, and no present sufficiently established to doubt.
For the time being at least there exists no need, as in
marriage, to work out compromises between opposing
sets of interest. The reawakening of passion seems all

but beyond belief, while the new zest for living is ample proof that the capacities of one's youth have only lain dormant, waiting for the person who could waken them to life. . . .

He also discovers another ability that he would hardly attempt to demonstrate at home—flirtation. No wonder he's excited, suddenly having all those long-buried talents released—nothing so appealing and challenging has happened in years. A new business venture is dull by comparison. What further justification is needed beside the reawakening of love that is taking place?

Now, of course, this is a most pitiable condition. Deception is paramount. To our momentarily reinvigorated friends it seems there is no tomorrow—no price to pay—but there is. To temporarily ignore this fact is to succumb to a will-o-the-wisp. The new affection is likely no more than a regressive need for self-affirmation.[4]

Many times a person will engage in an affair with someone at work, perhaps with a secretary or another employee. Reasons for this vary. One person may be using the affair to gain a new sense of power or control at work. Or perhaps the person has a feeling of pity or sympathy for the other man or woman. Sometimes it's simply a matter of enjoying the other person's company. Dwight Small describes other reasons for having an affair.

After years of counseling those involved in extramarital love affairs, I'm persuaded that many men and women find themselves in a grip of passion, with which reason cannot compete. Still others do not understand what's happening to them, locating the cause outside themselves. Of course, any romantic involvement is an exciting, pleasurable interlude in a life grown dull and monotonous with routine and familiarity. Perhaps there has been a failure to find success and adequate rewards in one's career. Perhaps there are fewer rewards in marriage—the married one has long since ceased nurturing. The affair is a tempting compensation for the love that's lost its luster. Per-

haps a man doesn't recognize a compelling need to
restore a slipping self-image and the temptation to satisfy that need through the faltering attention of a younger woman—a woman who at the time may be tempted
to participate in a romantically stellar performance
involving herself and an admired man.[5]

Another reason may be that, for the wife, the children's trials and triumphs have begun to take precedence over maintaining her appearance or tending to her husband's needs.
Often both he and she receive the leftovers. When the husband leaves in the morning his wife is rushing to get the children ready and to school on time and her attention is diverted
away from her husband. Or she herself is struggling to get to
work on time. Sometimes it's both! Then at the end of the day
she may be tired, harassed and involved with the children.
But at work the husband sees others who are "put together"
psychologically and physically, and he doesn't have to see
them or deal with them in the mundane activities of home.

Some use an affair as an attempt to get out of the marriage
by letting the spouse discover what is happening and then letting him or her file for divorce. This relieves the partner having the affair from the responsibility and the guilt of making
the initial move to terminate the marriage.

An affair may be generated by deep anger or outrage on the
part of a spouse who feels either abused, neglected or in some
way taken advantage of by the other. Thus the affair can
become a means of punishment and revenge.

Some use an affair to try to sustain a failing marriage by
supplementing the lack of intimacy with outside involvement.
Some even use the affair as a means of warming up a cold and
empty marriage. The person having the affair is aroused outside of his marriage, then returns to his spouse in the hope
that the arousal will carry over.

Those who are struggling with sexual dysfunctions,
incompatibility, or frustration may seek outside fulfillment.
Some women who question their femininity and ability to
attract a man move into affairs. Men who question their
potency and virility many times use affairs to prove their ability. Some say, "If my spouse cannot satisfy me, then someone
else can!" The involvement may be an attempt to deal with

advancing age and diminishing sexual capacity.

The yearning for romance is a common quest for many. For some the excitement of the unknown is very satisfying. Trapped feelings which come from a confining marital relationship are not usually present in an affair. Seeing the other person only during pleasant times adds to the enjoyment and erotic excitement. Doing something secret and forbidden with the potential of explosive consequences also adds to the excitement.

In discussing the causes of affairs, Lewis Smedes talks about external encouragement and internal encouragement. Our society and environment do little to encourage faithfulness. We live in an atmosphere which urges sexuality through media and the values and morals of so many. Sexual convenience is in effect for there is freedom from discovery and pregnancy. There are many sexually available people and more and more business contacts between the sexes.

Inner pressures or motivations are many and varied. Unresolved anger can push one into an affair in order to punish the partner. Self-hatred or a low self-opinion may lead to involvement. The person looks for someone who doesn't know him as well as his spouse. Or he has such a low opinion of himself that he readily accepts advances of most anyone.

Perfectionism compels some to want more than they have and to seek the impossible. They act out a fantasy but in time find it too disappointing.

Escape from life's pressures such as the job, in-laws, boredom, etc., contributes to some becoming involved. The promise of excitement and acceptance is an alternative to responsibly facing their own responsibilities.

Boredom itself can be a specific cause. As dreams fade or as the dull routine continues, the affair is sought as a replacement. Often couples grow apart because one chooses to grow emotionally and intellectually, leaving the other person behind. The gap widens and the one left behind is vulnerable.

Sexual deprivation leads some into a relationship with others. Lack of interest or a passive partner can create a frustration level which prompts one to seek other satisfaction. Lack of creativity or pleasure or an incapacitating illness also sets the stage for the affair.

Emotional deprivation is a major cause. The lack of need fulfillment and intimacy creates an intense vacuum. Failure to satisfactorily express one's needs and how they can be fulfilled, or refusing to be sensitive to each other's needs, contributes to alienation. Emotional pressure often precedes the movement toward physical satisfaction. The need for emotional intimacy is one of the greatest reasons for the affair. Wives have said, "What does he see in her? She's heavier than I am! I could understand a young, sexy doll, but *her*!" His response is, "She listens, cares and doesn't nag! That's more important than looks or sex."

Affairs begin not just for sexual reasons but to satisfy the basic need we all have for closeness, goodness, kindness, togetherness—what I call the "ness" needs. When these needs are not met on a regular basis in a marriage, the motivation may be to find a person who will be good to us, touch us, hold us, give us a feeling of closeness. Sexual fulfillment may indeed become an important part of an extramarital relationship, but the "ness" needs are, for most men and women I know, initially more important.[6]

Dr. Carlfred Broderick has talked with dozens of couples who have been fully committed to fidelity, yet found themselves involved in affairs. In most cases their involvement was centered around what he calls the three Rs of infidelity: resentment, rationalization and rendezvous.

Resentments which open the door to affairs can stem from anything. Failure to face and resolve them creates adulterous conditions. Factors such as insensitivity, excessive demands, neglect, lack of response and rejection contribute to infidelity.

Rationalization plays a large role in entering and perpetuating an affair. Faulty beliefs include, "It can never happen to me"; "Flirting is not dangerous and it means nothing." Dr. Broderick suggests:

But by far the most interesting and seductive form of rationalization is that which is rooted in virtue rather than vice. I am convinced that more people get themselves into the pain of infidelity through empathy, concern and compassion than through any base motive. The world is full of lonely and vulnerable people, hungry for a sympathetic ear and a shoulder to cry on. With a little help from rationalization, the sympathy leads smoothly into tenderness, the tenderness to the need for privacy, the privacy to physical consolation, and the consolation straight to bed.[7]

Attempting to help or console someone by being an available and sensitive listener may meet an unmet need for both individuals. "To be fair to yourself and to your marriage," Dr. Broderick suggests you ask yourself some questions:

1. Is my marriage currently in good repair? Are my most important affectional and sexual needs met within it? Do I feel warm, loyal and sexually attracted to my spouse? If there are problems between us, are we working together constructively to solve them, or are we letting resentments accumulate?

2. Do I find this other person attractive? Does he or she make me feel warm and giving? Do I find myself wishing that I could compensate this good person for all the hurt, pain and deprivation suffered at the hands of others? Would I feel the same way about someone who was twenty years older and a hundred pounds heavier and had a spouse who collected guns?

3. Do I feel that in order to be of real help to this person it is important for us to spend long hours together discussing his or her problems? Do I find myself relating my own marital problems in these sessions? Do I think about this person's problems when we are apart? Has he or she begun to assume a predominant place in my emotions? Do I find touching this person an important part of our relationship?

4. Does my spouse know where I am and what I am doing when I am with this person? If so, does that knowledge lead to approval or disapproval? Why are we not helping this person as a couple?[8]

Rendezvous often grows out of continual contact with another. Two people are brought together through circumstances such as working together, helping a neighbor, spending time in choir or church programs. An innocent get-together for coffee may begin a pattern of meetings which are mutually fulfilling to each. One man said, "We would meet on our break each day for coffee and just talk about innocent things. I really enjoyed the time. It was relaxed and I could be me. Soon we were sharing feelings and concerns. In two weeks we were in bed together. I just can't believe it's happening to me!"

The office environment is a prime setting for an affair. In this setting people look good, attempt to be at their best and are noticed by others. For many, going to the office is a welcome diversion. If the marriage is in trouble it's nice to be in an atmosphere of understanding and acceptance. Spending too much time in privacy with an attractive person of the opposite sex can lead to attractions. Then the offender rationalizes to cover any potential problems concerning the amount of time they spend together. If resentment and rationalization are present, then rendezvous can become planned.

Often there are many reasons for an involvement. But there are some who will say, "I don't know why. It just happened." Just as early warning signals occur for many problems in life—such as heart attacks or cancer—there are also telltale signs that a person may be vulnerable to an affair. Naivete can blind a person, which means that no one is completely safeguarded from involvement. "Affairs happen to others, not us" is the type of thinking which has led to disaster in many marriage relationships.

Warning Signs

One of the best ways to maintain fidelity in marriage and enhance the relationship is to ask *and* answer the question, "Am I leaning toward an affair?" We as believers are called to demonstrate fidelity, purity and integrity in our marriages. Drifting toward another can be a subtle and gradual process.

Some Christians are upset and offended by this question. Yet those who deny the possibility of ever engaging in an affair may be prime candidates. Denial of the warning signals may mean that if involvement occurs, it will be hard to stop.

Here are some of the warning signals suggested by individuals who have had an affair:

1. Regardless of the reasons that actually lead people into an affair, a drifting marriage often sets everything into motion; the feeling that you are simply going through the

motions of a marriage. You have quit actively participating in the marriage and little effort is exerted. Emotional energy is nonexistent in this marriage or it is diverted elsewhere.

2. A second indication is the creation of excuses to continually visit with someone in your work or social environment. People who have special feelings for another person begin to find ways to see the person—taking coffee breaks at a certain time, making excuses to drive a certain route or making phone calls over non-important items.

3. How do you handle repetitive contact with a particular person in a working, social or sporting situation? A married person needs to be able to deal successfully with frequent male/female contacts. Too much togetherness can lead to a desire for increased intimacy and, potentially, an affair. Two people who have sustained contact at work, choir, or committee work may fall into difficulty.

4. Do you find yourself preoccupied with your thoughts about another person? Scripture clearly states the importance of imagination (*KJV*): Genesis 6:5,6, "And God saw that the wickedness of man was great in the earth, and that every imagination of the thoughts of his heart was only evil continually. And it repented the Lord that he had made man on the earth, and it grieved him at his heart"; Proverbs 23:7, "For as he thinketh in his heart, so is he: Eat and drink, saith he to thee; but his heart is not with thee"; Isaiah 26:3, "Thou wilt keep him in perfect peace, whose mind is stayed on thee: because he trusteth in thee."

Preoccupation with daydreams and fantasies about another person is a definite danger sign. People stare out the window, go over and over their list of work to be done, burn dinners, forget appointments, etc. *Who* do you think about?

5. How and why a gift is exchanged with a friend of the opposite sex (and the type of gift exchanged) may indicate the development of intimacy. The selection and timing of gifts may reflect something about your relationship. Gifts can often become an expression or symbol of a person's feelings. The amount of *thought* and *time* that goes into the selection is another indicator.

6. How important has the telephone become in your relationship with a friend outside your marriage? Many who

became involved in an affair mentioned that continual use of the phone is an indication of too much involvement. The phone is fast, convenient but still personal enough to build a relationship.

7. Are you consciously putting yourself into situations where you can increase your chances of meeting someone who might become more than a friend? Those who are dissatisfied with their marriage and are not taking steps to build the relationship may begin searching in this manner.

8. What do our nonverbals say to others? Our body language makes up over 50 percent of our communication and can transmit messages which are quite obvious. If the eyes are the window to the brain, what message does the look in our eye give to another person? Do you ever send the message, "I'm interested" or "I'm available"? What do our touching, embracing and kissing mean, especially in Christian circles? What is the intent of our heart?[9]

Those who are involved in the affair take the brunt of rejection, anger and reaction when discovered. They are responsible for their actions regardless of the state of their marriage. They cannot project blame nor rest upon excuses for what has occurred. However, the victim or so-called blameless partner may not be as fault-free as it appears. There are many Christian marriages which are fertile ground for an affair. Lack of love, acceptance, need fulfillment, and sexual satisfaction with no desire on the part of the spouse to change and grow can set the gears in motion. Both man and wife need to ask the question, "What is my responsibility and what did I contribute to the cause of this affair?"

When affairs occur, other Christians spend an inordinate amount of time talking about what went wrong: "How could he (or she) be unfaithful?" "Their Christian testimony is ruined," etc. Instead of investing energy in speculation, gossip, and judgment, you need to ask yourself two questions: (1) In what way can I help and minister to the people involved? (2) How am I helping to create the conditions for an affair in my own life or my spouse's?

Mental Adultery
We are all prone to temptation. In fact, it would be safe to

say that we are all guilty of mental adultery at one time or another. And this is where so many affairs begin—in our mind.

Our thought life, our imagination is the spawning ground for our overt actions. And all of us struggle with our thought life. "And God saw the wickedness of man was great in the earth, and that every imagination of the thoughts of his heart was only evil continually" (Gen. 6:5, *KJV*). "Now the mind of the flesh [which is sense and reason without the Holy Spirit] is death—death that comprises all the miseries arising from sin, both here and hereafter. But the mind of the (Holy) Spirit is life and soul-peace [both now and forever]. [That is] because the mind of the flesh—with its carnal thoughts and purposes—is hostile to God; for it does not submit itself to God's law, indeed it cannot" (Rom. 8:6,7, *AMP*).

Loren Fischer describes this struggle:
> The steam of behavior is only visible proof that the fire of thought is boiling the water of emotion. A heavy lid may curb the steam of action but unless we curb the fire of thinking the heaviest lid possible will blow and high will be the blast of it. Obviously, therefore, we lose spiritual battles not by failing to restrain our actions with heavier lids, we are defeated because we do not change our flaming thoughts that boil the waters of emotion.[10]

Some advocate mental adultery as a means of tension release. The mental fantasy becomes a positive substitute for an actual affair. Unfortunately, feeding a fantasy can be the fuel which propels a person into direct action. Our behavior stems from thoughts. Energy spent in fantasy drains away time and effort which could be properly devoted toward the improvement of one's marriage. Fantasy has no demands or risks, and with it we fail to encounter real but imperfect people. Fantasy is an escape. Often a created fantasy is so unattainable and perfect that the here-and-now relationship with one's spouse seems to be lacking in comparison.

Two of the main factors which lead a person into an affair are unmet needs and a well-developed imagination. Note the process as illustrated in diagram 1:

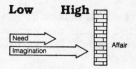

Diagram 1

In this first diagram we have a person whose imagination is at a high level. He spends time in detailed fantasy about people other than his spouse. But his need level is fairly low. This could be because his affection and love needs are met by his marriage partner.

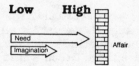

Diagram 2

In diagram 2 the need level is quite high, probably indicating a sterile relationship between the spouse for one reason or another. Fortunately, the imaginative process is not very highly developed. This lack of vivid fantasies directly focused upon another person is a safeguard.

The problem erupts when both imagination and needs are intense, diagram 3:

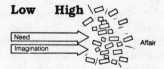

Diagram 3

The barrier between fidelity and infidelity begins to crumble when one's needs are not being met and when imagination of extramarital involvement is high.

Add to this the elements of resentment, rationalization, and rendezvous and a person becomes a prime candidate!

Dwight Small suggests that "we must commit our fantasies to the Lord for His review, for His commendation or censure."[11]

God created us as sexual beings. However, He did not create us to be attracted to just one person. We are sexually attracted to other people and this attraction promotes the development of emotions.

You cannot deny your sexuality nor your attractions. An attraction can be developed over a period of time with proper conditions; or it can occur almost automatically. Sexual responses and feelings should be accepted and not denied. Repressive denial can lead to volcanic explosion later on.

Is attraction then right or wrong? Is fantasy right or wrong? Is there a difference between lust and fantasy?

What Is Lust?

Is it possible to fully define lust? It *must* be defined and clarified for it is a misused and misunderstood word. In the Scriptures there are three Greek words and four Hebrew words for "lust" and to "lust after." Some of the usage of these words indicates the detrimental effects of lust.

In Psalm 78:18 the word *lust*, or *desire*, appears but with no sexual connotation. "And in their heart they put God to the test by asking food according to their desire" (*NASB*). Their problem was not one of hunger (a legitimate and often strong desire); God had provided food for those people. But they disdained His provision and demanded that God serve them from their own menu.

What about desire or lust in marriage? God is the creator of desire; it is good. But often we misuse and distort it. Since marriage is God's design, strong desire within marriage is not only natural, it is blessed. Even anticipative desire that precedes marriage is natural and blessed! This is the overwhelming conclusion a person finds after even a cursory reading of the Song of Solomon.

Jesus said, "You have heard that it was said, 'YOU SHALL NOT COMMIT ADULTERY;' but I say to you, that every one who looks on a woman to lust for her has committed adultery with her already in his heart" (Matt. 5:27,28, *NASB*). The words "to lust" are important. Is it lust to notice an attractive person of the opposite sex, or feel sexual arousal as you brush by a person, or have a fleeting sexual thought or wonder what it would be like with him or her? No, it is not!

Lewis Smedes sheds further light on this question.

> To "lust after" a person must have something to do with fanning desire into a flame of specific intent. And it probably has to do with a narrow focus on another person's body.
>
> There is a difference between the awareness of someone's sexual attractions and being dominated by a desire for that person's body. Jesus did not choose to draw a line between them. But we should know that there is a difference, so that we will be neither too quick to feel guilty nor too careless with our feelings. Attraction can become captivity; and when we have become captive of the thought, we have begun to lust. When the sense of excitement conceives a plan to use a person, when attraction turns into scheme, we have crossed beyond erotic excitement into spiritual adultery. There need be no guilt when we have a sense of excitement and tension in the presence of a sexually stimulating person; but we also need to be alert to where that excitement can lead.[12]

We will struggle with desire, temptation, and attraction. We will be in situations where we have friendships with those of the opposite sex. We are to heed the teaching of Scripture, accept our sexuality, remove ourselves from romantic settings with others and continually feed, nurture and maintain a need-fulfilling marriage. Remember, however, even a healthy marriage is not a guaranteed safeguard against an affair. We may be redeemed creatures but we are still fallen with a distortion of the image of God within us. We must commit not just our behavior to God but all our thoughts and feelings. An intimate, honest prayer life as a couple and a commitment to His Word are ways He gives us victory over temptation.

"There hath no temptation taken you but such as is common to man: but God is faithful, who will not suffer you to be tempted above that ye are able; but will with the temptation also make a way to escape, that ye may be able to bear it" (1 Cor. 10:13, *KJV*).

"In conclusion, be strong in the Lord—be empowered through your union with Him; draw your strength from

Him—that strength which His [boundless] might provides"
(Eph. 6:10, *AMP*).

"But thanks be to God, Who gives us the victory—making
us conquerors—through our Lord Jesus Christ (1 Cor. 15:57,
AMP).

Notes
1. Lewis Smedes, *Sex for Christians* (Grand Rapids: William B. Eerdmans
Publishing Company, 1976), pp. 168,169.
2. James H. Olthius, *I Pledge You My Troth* (New York: Harper and Row,
1975), p. 63.
3. Ibid., p. 63.
4. Dwight H. Small, *How Shall I Love You?* (New York: Harper and Row,
1979), pp. 118-120.
5. Ibid., p. 118.
6. Peter Kreitler with Bill Burns, *Affair Prevention* (New York: Macmillan
Publishing Co., 1981), p. 68.
7. Carlfred Broderick, *Couples* (New York: Simon and Schuster, 1979), p.
163.
8. Ibid., p. 164.
9. Kreitler, *Affair Prevention*, pp. 130-137, adapted.
10. Loren Fischer, unpublished manuscript.
11. Small, *How Shall I Love You?*, p. 127.
12. Smedes, *Sex for Christians*, p. 210.

Eight

The Healing of a Marriage

S ome of you will identify with this true story. A professional man sitting in my office discusses his gradual involvement with a young woman. It could happen to any of us.

"During this time a new woman came to work in our office. We struck up an acquaintance and began to talk each day over coffee. In time she began to share the problems in her own marriage and we found that we both were in a position of drifting away from our spouses. We actually found that we communicated better together than with our own spouses. We looked for reasons to be together—we shared similar interests and hobbies. I had no ulterior motives—no sinister plans but I enjoyed our time together as friends.

We saw each other every day for a few moments and once a week we went to lunch. In time I began to compare Elaine with my wife. I saw so many positives in Elaine. The more I compared the more defects I saw in my wife. Then one day it hit me. 'I was in love with another woman. Me! No! I'm a married man with three children. I'm chairman of our church board. This happens to others—why me! Why did I let myself get into this mess?' I felt confused. My work suffered—my relationships suffered. I tried to stop my involvement. Some weeks I didn't see Elaine that much. Other weeks I saw her every day. I had to! I had to!

"Last week it happened. We made love. I am so torn up right now! What do I do?"

Two hours later a couple sat across from me. Both husband and wife were angry and bitter. Both had been unfaithful. "He can never be trusted. I know this isn't the first time he's fooled around. And you can't believe the woman he took up with."

John sat there seething. Finally he glared at her and said, "I loved you once. But there's been no love in this marriage for the last several years. You yell at me about fooling around. What do you call your relationship with that 'special' friend! Deny that you've slept with him. And where did you meet him! Huh! In your couples group from the class. You can't even trust another Christian."

They both stopped talking and just looked at each other. They were angry but hurting. Finally Betty said, "I really don't want this marriage to end. Can anything be done? Is there any help?"

Affairs begin but they also come to an end. What are the results? The consequences?

Terminating the Affair

Three basic patterns occur when a person chooses to terminate an affair. First, the man (or woman) decides that this life-style is not what he wants. So he settles down with his wife (or husband) to build a much better marriage than they ever had before.

The second pattern occurs when the man (or woman) returns to his (or her) spouse but the spouse will not forgive him (or her). The problems which were there before the affair are not resolved. The security of the marriage is not established and in the future it will probably break apart again, perhaps for good.

The third pattern is that the involved spouse likes the new partner better than *the current* mate, and divorces.

Even though the majority of people I have seen involved in

affairs are committed Christians and know what the Word of God says about adultery, appealing to this knowledge does not usually cause them to stop the involvement. Appeals to family, mother, church, or even job security also have negligible effects.

Those involved will give many reasons for continuing: "I don't want to hurt the other person"; "He (or she) meets my needs so much better than my spouse"; "I've led him (her) to the Lord and we've developed a close and growing spiritual relationship"; "I've become a father to her children and can't leave them."

The disengagement process is difficult; but if the involved spouse is to become interested in and fall in love again with his own spouse, the affair needs to be broken immediately and completely. To be successful it cannot be ended slowly or piecemeal.

Often the person replies with, "But that will hurt her!" That is true, but that is part of the risk of an affair. Everyone gets hurt. Unfortunately, people don't think about that in advance. A spouse is at a distinct disadvantage as long as the affair continues. That which is new, exciting and doesn't have much of the daily mundane aspects of marriage attached to it usually takes precedence over the spouse. For the uninvolved partner to have a chance, the affair needs to come to an immediate halt.

But no matter what advice he receives, the person will probably not end the affair until he/she becomes uncomfortable with it or so dissatisfied and stressful that he/she begins to reconsider.

In cases where an affair is occurring (or often where couples are discouraged with their marriage) you will hear the excuse, "I don't love him anymore and I can't fall in love again," or "I don't think I ever loved her to begin with," or "I'm not sure it's worth trying." The best way to bring about a change in attitude is to use the resource "Love Life," by Dr. Ed Wheat. Many couples have been helped as a result of either listening to this tape series or reading the book.

The first indication that an affair is interrupting a marriage is usually a sense of uneasiness. In most cases the partner not involved in an affair becomes aware of some new intrusion into their relationship which increases the strain that is already there. The partner probes, questions and becomes increasingly suspicious. The secrecy and deception which accompany most affairs heightens the sense of romantic excitement for the involved person. But it also creates a greater sense of tension, guilt and pressure.

Typical Reactions by the Spouse

How might the offended person react to an affair? Here are some of the common mistakes a wife may make if she discovers her husband is having an affair:

1. She rails and denounces him, pushing him even further away. Anger is natural, but if it continues with no positive overtones toward her husband, he finds greater justification for what he is doing. This is one of the worst responses.

2. She tells as many others as possible. This may include his family, people at his work, and the children. This creates further alienation between them.

3. She will ask his family, closest friend or even his pastor to talk to him and straighten him out.

4. She either increases her sexual involvement with her husband in an attempt to win him back, or she eliminates sex entirely. For each couple, sex has a different meaning. Both the meaning and purpose of the decreased or increased activity must be explored and analyzed before a decision can be made concerning what might be best at this time.

5. She may go to see the other woman just to see what she looks like, to plead with her, or to verbally or physically attack her. If the woman is at her husband's work and the wife marches in to view her, this usually creates greater strain.

6. She may begin to campaign at home to make him suffer, or she may tell him to leave. Ordering a spouse to leave takes the responsibility away from him and may give him the excuse he has been looking for all the time. Or she may choose to leave, which usually is not in her best interest.

An affair is a breach of trust. It is often hard to regain trust when the affair is discovered, and some marriages are never the same. The offended spouse may never forgive. He or she may find it difficult to have intercourse afterwards because of thoughts of the spouse being in bed with another person.

Sometimes the guilty person becomes sexually unresponsive.

The violated trust is replaced by anger, rage, resentment, distrust, fear, doubt, cynicism and indifference. Since a commitment was broken, the sense of loyalty is shattered. One's sense of self-esteem is also lowered. As one woman said, "If he had chosen a younger attractive woman I could understand it. But why her? She's older than I am! What does he find so distasteful about me?"

The offended person needs to work through his/her feelings just as he/she would in any other crisis.

Throughout any type of marital crisis, but especially during an affair, the book *Living with Stress* by Lloyd Ahlem can be especially helpful. In most crises there is a sense of loss. The loss could be the relationship itself, one's sense of identity, one's values, etc. But whenever there is a loss there are fairly predictable stages that a person will go through as he seeks ways of resolving or adjusting to the crisis. The four stages or phases of a crisis are: (1) impact, (2) withdrawal and confusion, (3) adjustment, and (4) reconstruction and resurrection.

The impact phase is usually quite brief. This phase begins when the crisis becomes known. The offended spouse may be stunned. It could last a few hours to a few days. During this phase making decisions is a bit difficult, yet a person must make the fight-or-flight decision at this time. This decision is the question of staying and doing battle with the problem or running and ignoring it. During this phase people usually, in some way, make an attempt to search for what has been lost. Letting go is difficult for many of us, for it means losing control. Much of our security can be based upon being in control of our life, our situation, and events around us. Many have never really learned the meaning of trusting God and allowing Him to control and direct them. Even when a change involves a loss of something or someone who is detrimental to us, we will continue to search.

The second phase is withdrawal and confusion. The emotional level of a person in crisis drops to almost nothing. He suffers a numbness or depression—a worn-out feeling—which can last for days or weeks. Many deny their feelings at this time because anger might lead to guilt or shame.

The third phase is adjustment. Insight begins to emerge and positive attitudes develop. Some depression remains, but optimism is coming back. Detachment from the old is completed, and a search for the new has begun. Often at this time a person says that what he has learned through this experience he would never trade in spite of pain.

The final phase is reconstruction and reconciliation. In this stage the person has chosen between self-pity and hope. He establishes reattachments such as a new friend, activity, home, job, hobby, church. Second Corinthians 5:17, "If any man is in Christ, he is a new creature" (*NASB*), is a reality both spiritually and in the area of loss. Reconciliation is usually involved, for when crisis occurs, people around us are often hurt. When we go through a crisis we have a tendency to victimize others. Others feel our stress. Through confession or helpful gestures reconciliation can be accomplished.[1]

Becoming aware of the normality of this process makes a person much better able to deal with what is happening to him emotionally and in the relationship. It also gives him a greater degree of hope regardless of the outcome.

If a man 30 or over is the one involved in the affair, *Men in Mid-Life Crisis* by Jim Conway and *You and Your Husband's Mid-Life Crisis* by Sally Conway are helpful resources.

If the affair is continuing, the offended spouse's own possible contribution to it needs to be explored and necessary changes made. But no matter how loving and responsive the offended spouse becomes, there is no guarantee of what the partner will do.

To Tell or Not to Tell

Should the offended person be told? It is difficult to offer a blanket statement for every situation concerning whether to tell, how, when, and what the results will be. Ask 15 counselors and 15 ministers and you will find little agreement.

Many fear that confessing the affair may make things worse because there are no guarantees as to how the offended person will respond. Some people say, "If my spouse ever has an affair I don't want to know about it. I don't need that information to weigh upon me. My spouse would relieve his (her) guilt by doing that, and he/she could walk away feeling OK.

But what do I do with my anger, resentment, and feeling of being betrayed?"

In fact, some husbands or wives have been known to tell their spouses, "If you ever have an affair don't ever tell me about it. I don't want to have to get over that kind of hurt."

Some say that an affair should be shared only if the partner has the capability of working through the hurt and anger. Others fear the sharing as being potentially destructive. In some cases it seems the criterion for sharing, on the part of the person involved, is a guarantee that there will be no adverse reaction.

The meaning assigned to the affair by both partners is another factor to consider. If the marriage was sound and strong, the affair could have a less negative effect because of this strength. On the other hand, the affair could have a *more* negative effect because there seemed to be little rhyme or reason for its occurrence. If a person believes that an affair means the spouse no longer loves her, she will respond differently than if she believes the affair is a sexual involvement which will soon be over. Love, trust, and commitment can occur again, but it will take a great deal of work.

Even though each person involved in an affair must make up his own mind, to me it seems best to confess it to God and to one's spouse, realizing that there is no guarantee of acceptance, forgiveness, or restoration from the offended spouse. (But God always forgives and forgets.) If the affair is not confessed, and if it is discovered in the years to come, the effect could be even more upsetting. The one involved could spend years in fear that the discovery may occur, whereas the individual may have to live with his mate's wrath and suspicion for only a matter of weeks or months after the confession.

Just because a person is honest and confesses does not mean that instant reconciliation will occur. It will take time for the offended partner to move from the level of emotional involvement with the event to the level where he or she remembers that the affair occurred, but no longer feels emotional about it. It's like saying, "Yes, that happened. I know it did, but it no longer affects me. It's a fact of history, yet it has no emotional significance or effect. It's there, but we are progressing onward at this time, and I am not hindered nor is our relationship hurt by that event." This is, in a sense, forgetting. The fact remains, but it no longer entangles the person in its tentacles of control. The person involved needs acceptance and encouragement during the confession and reconciliation period.

The problem of an affair does not merely involve a person's feelings, nor does it bring with it a guarantee that everything will be all right once the affair is confessed. The issue is a theological biblical matter. Since there is some debate as to whether confession of sin should be only to God or to the offended party as well, consider John Stott's perspective from his book *Confess Your Sins:*

Some zealous believers, in their anxiety to be open and honest, go too far in this matter. To say "I'm sorry I was rude to you" or "I'm sorry I showed off in front of you" is right; but not "I'm afraid I've had jealous thoughts about you all day." Such a confession does not help; it only embarrasses. If the sin remains secret in the mind and does not erupt into words or deeds, it must be confessed to God alone. It is true that, according to the teaching of Jesus, "whosoever looketh on a woman to lust after her hath committed adultery with her already in his heart" (Mt. 5:28); but this is adultery in the sight of God and is to be confessed to Him, not to her. The rule is always that secret sins must be confessed secretly (to God), and private sins must be confessed privately (to the injured party).

Perhaps a word of caution may be written here. All sins, whether of thought, word, or deed, must be confessed to God, because He sees them all. "O Lord, Thou hast searched me, and known me. Thou knowest my downsitting and mine up-rising, Thou understandest my thought afar off. Thou compasseth my path and my lying down, and art acquainted with all my ways. For there is not a word in my tongue, but, lo, O Lord, Thou knowest it altogether" (Ps. 139:1-4). But we need to remember that men do not share the omniscience of God. They hear our words and see our works; they cannot read our hidden thoughts. It is, therefore, social sins of word and deed which we must confess to our fel-

low-men, not the sinful thoughts we may have har-
boured about them.[2]

Perhaps a guideline to follow would be to not confess until
the couple has worked sufficiently on their marriage so that it
is stabilized enough to handle the admission. This is where
the assistance of a Christian counselor can be so supportive.
Some couples may need the counselor's presence, when the
confession does occur, to ease the process. In many cases the
spouse has already had suspicions that an affair has
occurred, and it is not as much of a shock as expected.

Building a New Relationship

Once the partner has stopped the affair and has asked for
forgiveness, the couple will need to spend much time in counseling and in building a new relationship. The concept that
forgiveness is a process and not instantaneous must be
explored as well.

Forgiveness is not pretending. One cannot ignore the fact
that an event has occurred. Wishing it never happened will
not make it go away. What has been done is done, and becoming a martyr or pretending ignorance of the event does not
help the relationship. In fact, the lack of confrontation and
reconciliation may encourage the other person to continue or
repeat the same act or behavior.

Forgiveness is not a feeling. It is not a soothing, comfort-
ing, overwhelming emotional response that erases the fact
from one's memory forever. It is a clear and logical action that
does not bring up the past offenses and hurts but takes each
day a step at a time. Gradually there will be a bit less anger
and resentment and a bit more forgiveness until eventually
there is a wholeness once again.

Sexual transgressions sometimes occur. But, as with
other sins, God's grace is active and the presence of Jesus
Christ in a person's life can bring restoration and wholeness.
It will be your choice.

One of the assumptions which hinders us from forgiving
and making restoration is the belief that we can control neither our memory nor our thoughts. We can choose to dwell
upon the unfortunate event and the hurt which ensued, or we
can focus upon the repentance and restoration. If we say that

we cannot get over the hurt then we have chosen to keep it lodged in our mind; we are saying that the act is more important than the relationship with our partner. In our selective remembering we can either allow the continuous oozing and festering of a cancerous, terminal sore, or we can embrace the role of a healer. Healing is more than deciding not to be angry or hurt, withdrawn or silent. Healing means reconciliation. It involves empathy—carrying the other's hurt and making it our own. It means helping the other person become whole again. Healing is a beautiful experience. It means putting into operation our original marital ambition of bringing joy, happiness and encouragement to our partner.

David Augsburger describes the process of resentment and forgiveness:

> Resentment is a bulldog bite that clenches the teeth of memory into the dead past and refuses to let go. The past is slipping irretrievably away, and resenting determines to stop the universe until anger is satisfied.
>
> Painful experiences must be accepted emotionally as well as rationally. When the shock of an experience evokes more pain than can be accepted and assimilated at the moment of impact, then the emotional processing will follow, sometimes days later. This grieving and regrieving is a way of absorbing the full impact of what has occurred and coming to believe it with the heart as well as the head. When the loss is immense as in the . . . loss of a relationship or the rejection of love, months and sometimes years of mourning may be required before the loss is accepted emotionally. The heart has a memory too, and it must be allowed to feel its pain fully before releasing its hold on the past.
>
> When injury is an interpersonal one, the mourning takes the form of resentment which demands satisfaction from the other person. Inside the feelings of resentment there are demands, often many-layered demands.[3]
>
> What is demanded?
> Changing the unchangeable—

Turning time backward and undoing what has been done—

Continued suffering to atone for what has occurred.

Forgiveness says good-by to demands. Predictions of future failure which are the germs to prevent marital healing are cancelled.

We must let go!

Letting go is accepting one's humanity and recognizing one's powerlessness to force another or coerce satisfaction from the other, or to seduce the universe into functioning according to one's pretentious demands.

Letting go is relaxing one's grip on pain.

Most human pain is caused by holding on or holding back. Holding on to the past is like attaching one's nerve endings to an object outside oneself which is stuck, stationary. One must either stay with it to avoid pain, or feel one's nerve fibers slowly drawn into wire-like threads of torture. But since time moves inexorably forward, one cannot stay with the past. Pain results. An equal source of pain is found in the fantasy of holding back from the future. . . .

Letting go is necessary if one is to find release from the pain. Letting go allows one to flow forward again with the movement of time, to be present once more with oneself, one's companions, one's universe.[4]

Notes
1. Lloyd H. Ahlem, *Living with Stress* (Ventura, CA: Regal Books, 1978), chs. 3-7.
2. John R.W. Stott, *Confess Your Sins* (Philadelphia: Westminster Press, 1964), p. 27.
3. David Augsburger, *Caring Enough to Forgive* (Ventura, CA: Regal Books, 1981), p. 50.
4. Ibid., pp. 56,57.

Nine

The Season of Role Reversal

Growing older involves endings and beginnings; having to make changes and having some changes made for us. Not only do you change but your parents are changing too. And some of their changes may trouble you.

In later years a "role reversal" often occurs. The parent becomes the child and the child becomes the parent.

This role reversal comes about gradually. Slowly over a period of years you begin to realize that control has begun to shift from your parents to you. You find that responsibility is being transferred from their shoulders to yours, and now it's your duty to care for them.

You hear yourself saying things like, "You're sick, Mother? Have you called the doctor? Of course, you have the number. He's been your physician for 35 years. Alright, I'll call the office and tell them you're coming. You get ready and I'll be by to drive you down."

Or, "Did you take your medicine today? I know it tastes bad, but it's good for you and the doctor says you have to take it."

Or, "Dad, you shouldn't walk down to the post office without your sweater. Don't you know it's too cold for you this early in the morning?"

Or maybe you hear your dad say,"All the kids used to come here for the big Christmas dinner. I kind of miss that. Whose house are we going to this year?"

You find yourself taking the rake out of your dad's hands because it's "too much work for him." Or reconciling your mother's checkbook because "she never seems to get it right."

Then one day you're doing Mom's laundry, washing Mom's hair, telling her what she should eat and shouldn't eat. You get impatient as she dawdles around while you're waiting to take her shopping.

As one 48-year-old woman describes it, "It wasn't supposed to be like this. For years I was the one bathed, dressed, fed, consoled, taught, disciplined, ordered around, cared for, and every need anticipated. I patiently waited for my turn to come when I could command and be independent. Now that it's here, why am I so sad?"

The first time I read this tears came to my eyes. I could see that my mother too is changing. She has always been so strong, decisive and independent. Born in 1900 she has possibly seen more change in her lifetime than most living or dead. She emigrated from South Dakota to California in 1919 in a dilapidated car that quit in the desert. She and her first husband lived in a shack in the Hollywood hills until they constructed their first home. During that time she walked several miles a day to work. Eventually she had four homes there and, for decades, rented them out. She survived the demise of two husbands; she traveled in her seventies to Europe, the Holy Land, Russia and all over the U.S.

When I was born, Dad was 50 and she was 38. I was asked by my friends, "What is it like to have old folks for parents?" I never thought of them as old. They were very active and more involved with me as parents than my friends' parents. They encouraged me, pushed me, argued with me and believed in me. When I was young I was dependent upon them. Now Mom is more and more dependent upon me. As I see the changes taking place in her I have a vast surge of emotions. Sometimes I handle the changes and on other occasions I struggle within myself.

When you have been strong and capable and independent you don't want to admit your incapabilities. We as children must be careful not to take away their freedom, their hope, their dreams (realistic or unrealistic), their usefulness and sense of worth. For if we do we eliminate their will to live.

The more you tell them what they cannot do, the more they may seek to prove to you and to themselves they can. Or else they wither and retreat. You may move into the role of parenting them, but this must be done as a helper. You must avoid being short, angry, condescending, judgmental.

When we see our parent behaving in such a changed or dependent manner we sometimes become angry and impatient with them. Why? How strange a reaction toward a loved one! Perhaps we cannot handle their increased limitations and are reminded that their time with us is becoming less and less. We have been used to them being strong and we feel, "This isn't right. They shouldn't be acting this way. This shouldn't be happening to them. Not my mom. Not my dad."

Perhaps it reminds us that we will someday change as they are changing. How do we feel about that? Perhaps our impatience and irritation are a defense against fear for them and for ourselves. We do not like what we see happening but we can do nothing about it. Life is following its pattern. At this time in life we perhaps have greater emotional control; we need to exercise it. Their life is limited. They may repeat the same incident again and again. But perhaps what they are repeating is the only thing of consequence that has happened to them lately.

Coping with our parents' increasing infirmities is a responsibility and a privilege most of us will eventually experience. How will you handle it? What does it do to your own thoughts of the future? Upon what are you basing your own sense of usefulness?

How you handle these changes in your parents may be determined by your past involvement with them. Memories of past experiences will affect present actions and feelings. If you have experienced loving, giving parents you will find it easier to respond positively. You respect them and can accept their weaknesses. You may hurt more, however, as you grieve for their limitations. If you did not experience love and acceptance as a child, but rather ridicule or abuse, you may have negative feelings. You may feel anger and resentment at having to help someone who did little for you. At times you may feel neutral or ambivalent.

No matter how you feel you will experience mixed emotions. Some of the interactions with your parents will be positive; others will involve conflict and negative feelings.

Dr. Stephen Cohen and Bruce Michael Gans have written an excellent book entitled *The Other Generation Gap*, to help children and their aging parents. In their conclusion they suggest basic principles of aging which both we and our parents face.

The Process of Growing Old

If your parents are elderly, the very fact that they have lived to their seventies or eighties indicates that they still have many physical and emotional strengths.

The productiveness of those above seventy is amazing. Michelangelo began his artistic masterpiece on the Sistine Chapel at 76! Hudson Taylor, the great missionary, worked until he was 79. Agatha Christie continued writing her novels well into her eighties. Joma Kenyatta became the first president of Kenya in his seventies. Arthur Fiedler, the conductor, began to cut down on conducting the Boston Pops at the age of 82. Instead of 194 concerts a year he conducted only 164! And the list goes on and on. Strengths and giftedness exist and can be used. It will be important to discover and reinforce those strengths instead of focusing upon what is wrong and what cannot be accomplished.

New illnesses and weaknesses will continuously be brought to your parents' attention. Remember that these will be frightening and depressing. As parents grow older their problems will become more obvious. The human body will show the many years of living. An ache to an older person means much more than to someone younger. It is a greater threat. They worry about body functions which we take for granted. You may hear them talk about bowel movements, urinary tract problems, eyesight ("they make the print smaller each year"), hearing loss, dentures, aching joints, etc. All of these symptoms remind them of their dwindling capacities and of the inevitable. Their ability to read, play, exercise, engage in sex are all reduced. Many have chronic illnesses. Of those close to 65, about half of the men and 40 percent of the women live with some activity limitation. (Remember that the other half does not; and many are extremely active!)

Your parents' physical and emotional health is not going to improve with time; it is going to deteriorate. This is painful to accept but the reality of it must be faced for their sake as well as yours. By accepting this fact you can help them set realistic goals. And when you try to find ways to help them function with their infirmities, follow those which help them maintain their daily routine as much as possible.

Besides deteriorating health, older people for the most part also suffer economic deprivation. Because of limited savings, forced retirement and little ability to supplement their income, more than half of the men over 65 bring in less than five thousand dollars a year.[1]

One thing that probably will not change are your parents' old habits. However, they may become more pronounced. These habits are ingrained and are a link to the past. Attempting to change them would mean another loss in their perception. Your own habits will intensify with age too. Which habits or behaviors do you want to continue? Which have you already tried to change? I talk to many individuals in their thirties and forties who believe it is impossible for them to change at their particular time of life! If you believe that, why try to change your elderly parents? (The belief that you cannot change in your thirties or forties is, in fact, erroneous! If a person desires to change and seeks help it *is* possible.)

The elderly suffer a great deal emotionally and physically when they face dramatic change. Change for them has a different meaning than it did when they were younger; it is no longer a novelty or a time for growth. It means another part of their world has crumbled and been destroyed. It is another grim reminder of their deterioration. They need help to cope with any change. We often confuse what is best for them with what is best for us.

Prolong the independent functioning of your parents by whatever combination of means is necessary. Make use of all resources and agencies so they do not become a burden to themselves or to you. Help them discover others their own age. Use community agencies and the many programs that some offer. If your church has no definite ministry to the elderly, why don't they? (For practical help with this issue of community resources see pages 356-366 of *The Other Generation Gap*.)[2] Confinement to a nursing home should be considered as a last resort.

Determine the level of your own involvement and explain it to your parents. But first determine whether your involvement is based on love and concern or guilt and obligation. Parents need to be seen as mature adults and treated as such. When you respond out of duty there is a price to pay. Some feel, "My parents took care of me when I was a child, and now since they have needs it is my duty to take care of them." Who would take care of them if you were not around? Equating your duty to your parents with parents' duty to their children makes them less of an adult.

Fear and Loneliness

Fears are multiple among the elderly. They fear death, getting sick, and being assaulted. They also have a fear of falling, fear of breaking a bone and not having it heal. They also fear losing money, losing love, being abandoned, being "put in a home." They fear dying alone.

Some feel their greatest struggle is loneliness. Today 80 percent of the elderly live in a home with their spouse or live alone. Fifty years ago they lived in a home with other members of the family. Our country has shifted from rural to city population. Many parents live in homes or apartments where contact with others is almost totally limited. How do they deal with their loneliness? They may phone you constantly or they may not phone at all. They insist that you visit them but then decline your offer with, "Oh, you're so busy, don't bother." They complain of having a disease but in reality have none. They lose weight or they gain weight. They change doctors frequently. These behaviors often indicate loneliness. And they get very lonely.

An 84-year-old woman, living in a rundown apartment in Los Angeles, sent this message to the *Los Angeles Times:* "I'm so lonely I could die—so alone. I cannot write. My fingers and

hand pain me. I see no human beings. My phone never rings
. . . I hear from no one . . . never have any kind of holidays, no
kind. My birthday is this month. . . . Isn't anyone else lonely
like me?. . . I don't know what to do." She enclosed some
stamps and a one-dollar bill hoping that someone would
either call her or write to her. When a newsman called her she
burst into tears.

Ira Tanner writes:

"Loneliness has a way of infecting every fiber of our
being: our hopes, ambitions, dreams, vitality, desires,
wants, as well as our actual physical bodies. Eating
and sleeping are frequently affected. Obesity and greed
may well be symptoms of loneliness, although a loss of
weight can also be traced to despair that goes with a
feeling of being of no importance or worth to anyone,
not even to ourselves. The misery of loneliness may
manifest itself in aches (imagined or real) in the body.
Weakness in the legs is not uncommon, stemming
from the heavy burden of fear that we are carrying on
our backs. Stooped shoulders, turned-down corners of
the mouth, a slow and painful walk, silence and withdrawal—all bear testimony to the disease. "I hurt deep
down in the pit of my stomach, my arms and shoulders
ache to be held tight . . . to be told that I am really loved
for what I am," said one woman.[3]

Lord Byron helps us feel the full impact of this aloneness
the elderly feel in one of the stanzas of "Childe Harold":

What is the worst of foes that wait on age?
    What stamps the wrinkle deeper on the brow?
To view each loved one blotted from life's page,
    And be alone on earth, as I am now.

Feeling lonely is like being isolated even though others are
close at hand. A songwriter describes it like this:

If I were a cloud, I'd sit and cry,
If I were the sun, I'd sit and sigh,
But I'm not a cloud, nor am I the sun,
I'm just sitting here, being no one.

If I were the wind, I'd blow here and there,
If I were the rain, I'd fall everywhere,
But I'm not the wind, nor am I the rain,
I'm just no one—feeling pain.

If I were the snow, I'd fall oh so gently,
If I were the sea, waves would roll o'er me,
But I'm not the snow, nor am I the sea,
I'm just no one—and lonely.[4]

The clue to what loneliness really is can be found in the
line from Psalm 142, "No man cared for my soul"(v.4, *KJV*).
Loneliness is the feeling of being cut off from other people,
deserted, or banished from their company. It is not the mere
fact of being physically alone; it is the result of a breakdown in
the emotional giving and receiving between people.

Although loneliness afflicts many old people it does not
affect all of them. However, *none* of them should have to suffer
with loneliness if they prepare for it while they are younger.
Perhaps some loneliness is at the germination stage in your
own life. Becoming aware of some of these beginnings could
help you deal with them before they become acute; or knowing
the causes of loneliness could help you help your aging friends
or relatives in their time of loneliness. Following are some of
the causes of loneliness.

First, there can be *geographical reasons* for loneliness.
When aged persons become ill and are hospitalized they are
often placed in institutions or hospitals miles away from their
homes. As a result they feel cut off. They miss their friends
who probably cannot come to visit very often. They may miss
the climate they are familiar with, and they especially miss
their home. The new routine of the hospital or nursing home
makes them miss the routine they were accustomed to in
their own surroundings.

Another cause of loneliness is being surrounded by people
who speak a foreign *language*. There are older people in our
society who may have been in the United States for many
years but who still have not mastered the English language.
They feel isolated and alone when they are around those who
do not speak their native tongues.

Cultural differences can cause loneliness; living in a new place where his/her familiar customs are not practiced. This is especially true if he is from another country and is confined to a nursing home in a strange land.

Illness is an often-experienced cause of loneliness. The pain of the illness can bring a feeling of separation and isolation. We do not respond as well when we are sick, and acute physical stress can leave us feeling helpless and totally dependent upon others. Think of the loneliness and feeling of isolation you would have if you lost your eyesight, hearing, or your ability to get around on your own. Think how it would be to be cut off from your radio or television because of permanent loss of a body function. How would you fill hour after lonely hour?

The longer a person lives the more of his relatives, friends and possessions he loses. He/she is often heard talking about the past, about those things and people that are no longer around. This is described as *loss loneliness.*

Impending death can cause a great loneliness among the aged. With the loss of so many people and things they held so dear, and nothing coming in to fill the void, their losses become greater and death becomes more fearful. Aged people have a number of fears about death: they fear dying alone, severe pain, becoming paralyzed by a stroke, dying in a strange place, being confined for the rest of their lives.

Coping with Death

Being *widowed* causes loneliness. The loss of a mate through death is probably the most devastating experience an elderly person endures. To suddenly lose the one who knows you backward and forward, and with whom you share a storehouse of memories, creates many problems; but perhaps the hardest problem to adjust to is loneliness. The now departed mate was needful in a number of ways. First, he/she was always around to interact with. Now that source of interaction is gone. The widowed person enjoyed and misses the mate.

Second, the widowed person no longer feels that he/she is the object of another person's love. If a woman depended heavily upon her husband's reinforcement of her sense of worth, she feels her loss more intensely than she would if she felt loved by many.

Third, the widowed person's companion is now gone. The intensity of companionship is not easily replaced. Adjusting to living alone produces loneliness. The widow or widower must learn to live in a home without a mate. He/she must learn to do things alone and to enjoy them without being able to share with another person. A widow no longer has someone to take part of the work load, or do tasks she could not do or did not like to do. She depended upon the one who is no longer there.

The widowed feels sadness because of the loss of a life-style he/she enjoyed with the other person. Perhaps they bowled together or played golf or went to dinner parties together. But now the one left behind loses the desire to participate in these activities. Often a widow is no longer invited to activities because it was her husband's contacts that made these invitations possible; perhaps the activities are for couples only. Our society, even in our churches, are for the most part couple-oriented.

Another reason why a widowed person feels the intensity of loneliness could be his/her inability to make new friends. Perhaps he/she lacks the skill or opportunity to establish new relationships.

Grief itself brings a sense of loneliness. Ralph Cokein describes his own experience of loneliness in grief in an article, "A Loneliness I Never Expected":

We had shared so many years together, we had shared so many wonderful and exciting experiences, we were so much in love and such inseparable companions, the very idea that one of us would die and leave the other alone and bereaved seemed so remotely distant that we refused to entertain it and spoil our fun.

Come the first day of summer (what irony!) she will have been dead two years.

I miss her terribly and I have agonized—nearly to the point of self-destruction.

I find no purpose in living, though I have been told that purpose will eventually manifest itself. There are no fond expectations, no stimulating goals, no promising future.

Everything seems different—even the newspaper

she loved so much and the newsmagazine that could disturb her routine if it arrived a day late. We frequented so many places I am constantly reminded of her; the music we shared I cannot bear to hear now. What anguish to come home night after night to an empty apartment devoid of her warmth and radiance.[5]

How are *you* affected when one of your parents dies? What is the impact upon you as the child? Not only do you have to deal with your own grief, but also the grief of your surviving parent, and that of your own children as well. You may resent having to be the "strong" person at this time.

When your parents die, your own fear of death becomes exaggerated. Sometimes an intense fear of dying triggers an obsessive preoccupation with your own health. Most of us feel more vulnerable, as if our parents were a shield standing between us and death; now that the parents are gone, we are next—and it can happen at any time; if one parent is still alive, we can maintain the illusion that death is an orderly event which we are protected against by someone else. This is another childhood protective device which we retain well into adulthood to preserve our illusion of safety.

The grief and the loneliness involved in losing a loved one is especially intense. Have you experienced this yet in your life? I said yet because at some time all of us will. How will you cope with the loneliness of grief? How can we help others through this time of grief and feeling of loss? If you have never discussed this with your spouse or another person, do so now.

How are you equipping yourself for becoming elderly? Those who handle old age well are those who handle their own needs with balance and self-assurance earlier in life. Those who are independent and resourceful do well in old age. Of course you must begin to be independent and resourceful before you need to be, before old age.

Factors which indicate a successful adjustment are the following:

1. Keeping in contact with others.

2. Reading extensively about the various changes which come from old age.

3. Maintaining a balanced diet; the changes you encoun-

ter will be less frightening and disturbing if you are physically healthy and aware that the disturbances you are experiencing are normal.

4. Maintaining as much independence as possible.

5. Anticipating changes and losses in advance and seeking out substitutes.

6. Building a life of service to others.

7. Discovering your strengths and continuing to build upon them.

8. Accepting your aging whether your are 35, 45, or 60. Live with the reality of the present, anticipate the future and let go of the past. If you deny aging you are afraid of it. Denying aging is counter to the purpose of God. God is with us and for us at every age of life. There is provision for every age of life in God's Word.

Psalm 23:6: "Surely goodness and lovingkindness will follow me all the days of my life, and I will dwell in the house of the Lord forever" (*NASB*).

Psalm 92:12-14: "But the godly shall flourish like palm trees, and grow tall as the cedars of Lebanon. For they are transplanted into the Lord's own garden, and are under his personal care. Even in old age they will still produce fruit and be vital and green" (*TLB*).

Isaiah 46:4: "I will be your God through all your lifetime, yes, even when your hair is white with age. I made you and I will care for you. I will carry you along and be your Savior" (*TLB*).

When Jesus said, "I came that they might have life, and might have it abundantly" (John 10:10, *NASB*), He did not have an age limitation!

Old age may seem a long way off now, but it will be here all too soon. Preparation begins now. Some feel they will never live to be old. But who really knows? Many are determined that they will not be like their parents when they grow old. Perhaps not, but you will follow their pattern unless you begin making plans and changes now. You cannot escape from many of the problems mentioned here. Attitudes, values and behavior change can occur only if you determine your goals for these changes, develop a plan to bring them about and then consistently work toward them. This involves determination, flexibility, willingness to endure the pain of growth and relying upon the resources of God through His Word. After all, doesn't the Scripture say that the Christian walk is a life of faith? Isn't it to be a walk all of our life?

Notes

1. Carol Flax and Earl Ubell, *Mother, Father, You* (New York: Wyden Books, 1980), p. 30, adapted.
2. Stephen Cohen and Bruce Michael, *The Other Generation Gap* (New York: Warner Books, Inc., 1978), part 4.
3. Ira J. Tanner, *Loneliness—The Fear of Love* (New York: Harper and Row Publishers, 1973), p. 11.
4. Linda Rich, "No One." Assigned to InterVarsity Christian Fellowship of the U.S.A., used by permission, 1970.
5. Ralph Cokein, "A Loneliness I Never Expected," *New York Times*, March 24, 1972.

Ten

The Final Season: A Time to Die

The older we grow, the stronger looms the reality of death. You may have already experienced or soon will face the death of a close family member or friend, and begin to think more about your own death. A major task of mid-life is coming to grips with the fact that you will not always be around and that you could die sooner than you think or wish! Such thoughts bring a certain feeling of helplessness because death is something you cannot control.

Mortality is an issue which most of us want to avoid. Even we Christians, who say we have no fear of death, would still like to avoid the process of dying. Man denies death, runs from it, ignores it and represses it. Remember the story of the fear of death?

Death was walking toward a city, and a man stopped Death and asked, "What are you going to do?"

Death said, "I'm going to kill 10,000 people."

The man said, "That's horrible."

Death said, "That's the way it is. That's what I do."

So the day passed. The man met Death coming back, and he said, "You said you were going to kill 10,000 people but 70,000 were killed."

Death said, "I only killed 10,000. Worry and fear killed the others."

Ernest Becker in *The Denial of Death* says, "The idea of death, the fear of it, haunts the human animal like nothing else; it is a mainspring of human activity—activity designed largely to void the fatality of death, to overcome it by denying in some way that it is the final destiny for man."[1]

Robert Burton said, "The fear of death is worse than death."

The Scriptures have much to say about death:

Psalm 116:15: "His loved ones are very precious to him and he does not lightly let them die" (*TLB*).

Hebrews 9:27: "It is destined that men die only once, and after that comes judgment" (*TLB*).

Revelation 21:4: "He will wipe away all tears from their eyes, and there shall be no more death, nor sorrow, nor crying, nor pain. All of that has gone forever" (*TLB*).

What is death? It is the permanent, irreversible cessation of vital functions of the body. But not all functions stop at the same time. It used to be that the lack of heartbeat was considered final evidence of death but now the attention has shifted from the heart to the brain for a reliable indication of when death has occurred.

Joe Bayly says that death is a wound to the living.

Why We Fear Death

Why is it that we fear death so much? Why do we deny death and shrink from even discussing it? We criticize the Victorians because of their attitude toward sex, but, unlike us, they were very aware of and dealt openly with death. Why do we fear death? There are several reasons.

We fear physical pain and suffering. We fear the unknown. We fear leaving loved ones and friends. Today 80 percent of our society dies away from home or familiar surroundings. This in itself creates fear because we do not want to be alone when we die.

Cyrus L. Sulzberger, in his book *My Brother Death*, says, "Men fear death because they refuse to understand it." In order to understand death we must deal with our fears of death. In her book *Mourning Song*, Joyce Landorf says:

Here, then, is part of the answer as to why death frightens us so much. While, as a Christian, I know Christ has removed the sting of death and death can never kill me for eternity—death still exists. It is still fearfully ugly and repulsive. I probably will never be able to regard, imagine, or fantasize death as being a loving friend.

Whenever and wherever death and dying connects with us—no matter how strong we are prepared for it— it still slides and slithers into our lives and freezes us with fear. Such is the nature of death.[2]

Death separates us from familiar people, places and things. We enter into a journey in which there is no hope of a return visit. We cannot write, phone or come back.

We are fearful because the time of death is uncertain even when we are stricken with a terminal illness. A person is apparently healthy one day and dead the next. Death can be peaceful and pleasant or violent and horribly repulsive and disfiguring.

We fear death because it is an unknown. We really don't know what it is like to die even when people tell us their "near death" experiences.

We are all a terminal generation. Life is terminal. From the minute we are born we are engaged in the process of dying. In middle age some people begin to realize that "time is short," others feel that "time will soon be up." The awareness that time is short can help us evaluate what is important to us and what we want to do with the rest of our time.

Each of us has a sensitivity to our length of life and the fact that we will die. How aware are you of your approaching death? J. William Worden and William Proctor discuss three examples of *Personal Death Awareness*.

1. Very Low Personal Death Awareness. Sam was a fifty-five-year-old man who had not been able to tolerate funerals, wakes, or hospitals. Admitted to the hospital and diagnosed as having advanced terminal stomach cancer, he refused to accept the diagnosis. Though he lost weight and strength, he insisted he would be back to work soon. He refused to affirm his religious beliefs

or accept the ministries of his priest. He failed to prepare his wife for living alone. He did not discuss plans for funeral and burial. He died without a will. Worden and Proctor conclude, "Sam's life-style—his previous stress on the importance of marital love, efficiency in his daily affairs, and a firm religious faith—was abandoned in his death style of denial."

2. Very High Personal Death Awareness. Lisa, a school teacher, twenty-seven years of age, was frequently preoccupied with her own death. Bad dreams of death and anxieties occasionally caused her to miss work. She refused to believe that a previous case of hepatitis (a fairly common liver disease) was really cured, and she returned to the hospital frequently for additional liver tests. She would refuse to believe the negative results and thought she was going to die of this illness in the near future. Friends were turned off by her fear of a shortened life. She found herself angry and alone.

Lisa turned to psychotherapy and discovered the reason for her preoccupation with death. Her father had died when she was thirteen. He was an alcoholic and had been estranged from the family. When he died, the family expressed their anger at him by a quick, private funeral and cremation, spreading the ashes "to the winds." Though Lisa, the youngest child, objected, the family proceeded with these plans. She felt angry and hopelessly frustrated.

Therapy helped her get in touch with her obsessive fear of death. Her fear was that she would end up like her father, dead with no one caring. By discovering the roots of her fear, she brought her Personal Death Awareness to a more manageable level.

3. Moderate Personal Death Awareness. Jack was a thirty-year-old husband and father of six with a terminal kidney ailment. He received every medical treatment available, including two kidney transplants, neither of which worked because of his body's susceptibility to infection. Though he hoped for another donor he finally realized there would be no

more. His first reaction was irritability. Then this
phase passed and he assumed a realistic attitude
toward his limited life span. He began to discuss his
situation frankly with his wife and they found themselves able to cry together. This in turn opened up communication so that they could make plans for the present and the future. They discussed every relevant
topic—mortgage payments, driving lessons for his
non-driving wife, domestic chores, and financial
responsibilities. He told her he wanted a simple burial
to save money for the children's education. He
expressed the desire that his body be used to serve; he
wanted his eyes donated to people who needed them.
He and his wife expressed their love for each other and
communicated his coming death to their children.
When he died, the children decided to take turns caring for their father's cemetery plot.[3]

Where do you see yourself in these examples? Which of
these do you identify with the most? The least? What do you
fear most about death? If you are married how do you think
your death will affect your mate? Would you or have you
encouraged your spouse to remarry after you die? Have you
talked with your spouse about your feelings concerning
death? How long would you like to live? What type of death do
you fear the most? Have you thought of how you will handle
being a widow or widower?

Mourning the Death of a Spouse

How do you survive the death of a spouse? During your
mourning period you will probably find yourself denying the
reality of death, like a bad dream from which you will awaken.
Even with a minimum of denial you will experience grief as
memories recur of poignant moments together, the voice that
will never be heard, the skin that will never be touched, and
the look, the gesture that will never be seen again. Each memory you cherish hammers home the painful message of finality. And it has to be hammered home time and time again to
be believed.

It is absolutely essential to bear the pain of the mourning
period if you are to stay in touch with yourself. Any pocket of

hope that your loved one's death is only a dream falsifies reality and closes off a section of your mind. The pain of remembering and longing and realizing what can no longer be destroys any hope of cheating death. And it thereby keeps you open and alive.

No matter what form your mourning takes, after the death of a spouse the world is a different place. For a period of time it is emptier or lonelier or less meaningful. Some may see it as cruel, harsh, ugly and a stupid place to be. The hypocrisy, the petty values of everyday life become glaringly apparent in contrast. Touching other human beings deeply becomes life's meaning for many mourners, while others return to some sort of a religious involvement. Still others foreswear religion as useless—"a good God wouldn't let this happen to me."

When you lose a loved one, what will you experience? Your first response is the shattering, devastating shock that comes with news of the death. This shock is followed a month or so later by intense suffering and extreme loneliness. Sometime during the first or second year a slow, gradual strengthening and healing of your mind and emotions takes place. For most people the grief process can take up to two years.

The stages of grief that you will pass through are normal and can be immediate or postponed. It is vital for you to do your grief work.

The first stage is *shock and crying.* This outlet is normal. Some uninformed and mistaken Christians may make comments such as, "Stop your crying. After all your husband is with the Lord now." Such comments are not helpful and are quite insensitive. Psalm 42:3 states, "My tears have been my food day and night" (*NASB*). You need to cry.

The second stage is *guilt.* This is almost a universal phenomenon. Statements or reactions such as, "If only————" "Why didn't I spend more time with him?" and "Why didn't we call in another doctor?" are often made.

Hostility is the next typical response you may experience. Anger at the doctors for not doing more; anger at the hospital staff for not being more attentive; anger even at the person who died. A husband might react by saying, "Why did she die and leave me with three children to care for?" Then guilt and remorse set in because of his angry feelings. If you know ahead of time that these reactions are normal, grief will be a little more acceptable.

Restless activity is the next stage. A bereaved person begins a lot of activities but quickly loses interest and switches to other projects. It may be hard for you to return to your regular routine.

In the fifth stage your *usual life activities lose their importance*, bringing further depression and loneliness. These activities were important only because they were done in relationship with the one you have lost.

The last stage is *identification* with the deceased. You may continue the projects or work of the deceased. For example, a wife may carry on her husband's unfinished hobby. A husband may continue to add to the house, which had really been his wife's project. The person begins to do what the deceased did and to do it the way he/she did it. In some cases people begin having the same symptoms or pains the deceased experienced. If the husband's back hurt extensively while he was ill the wife finds her own back starting to ache. All of this is just part of the identification process.

Ten Stages of Grief

Granger Westberg, in his book *Good Grief,* suggests that there are 10 stages of grief the normal person must pass through.[4] If you know what these 10 stages are perhaps it will help you to understand some of your feelings when you go through grief.

1. Shock. This is the temporary anesthesia, the temporary escape from reality. Allow other people to be near you to help you. But don't let them take away from you what you can do for yourself. The sooner you have to make some decisions and deal with the immediate problem the better off you will be.

2. Emotional release. Cry over the loss of your loved ones. Talk about your grief.

3. Depression and loneliness. This stage will also pass. Keep up your daily routine and get out of the house. See other family members for a brief period of time and engage in some form of physical activity; this will help lift the depression.

4. You may have some symptoms of distress, such as panic, anxiety or even physical symptoms. Some of these

could be due to repressed emotions.

5. Panic about yourself or the future may set in. This is because death is always in your mind. You begin to fear your own death or the death of someone else.

6. A sense of guilt about the loss. You need to talk through these feelings with another person.

7. Hostility and resentment. When you are in grief you become angry easier, quicker and at people and situations that normally do not arouse anger.

8. Inability to return to your usual activities. Unfortunately, people around a mourner tend not to talk about the deceased. They may remember an important time in the person's life or a humorous incident, but they refrain from talking about it in the presence of the remaining partner. And yet if they did so they would make it much easier for the mourner. Talking about fond remembrances is healthy.

9. Gradually hope will begin to return. Rabbi Joshua Liebman, in his book *Peace of Mind*, wrote an excellent chapter on "Grief's Slow Wisdom" which speaks most effectively to the temptation not to return to normal activities. Liebman said, "The melody that the loved one played upon the piano of your life will never be played quite that way again, but we must not close the keyboard and allow the instrument to gather dust. We must seek out other artists of the spirit, new friends who gradually will help us to find the road to life again, who will walk that road with us."[5]

10. The final stage is the struggle to affirm reality. This does not mean that the person becomes his old self again; however any person experiencing grief comes out of it a different person. Depending upon how he responds, he can come out as a stronger or a weaker individual.

Grief Work

A mourner needs to complete his "grief work." Grief work means (1) emancipating oneself from the deceased (read 2 Sam. 12:22,23), (2) adjusting to life without the deceased, and (3) making new relationships and attachments.

Grief work is the reviewing by the bereaved of his life together with the deceased. This involves thinking about the person, remembering dates, events, happy occasions, special occasions, looking at photos, and fondling trophies or items important to that person. In a sense, all of these activities are involved in the process of psychologically burying the dead.

Our tendency many times is to deny the bereaved his opportunity for grief work. We may come into the widow's home and find her looking at pictures in her husband's workshop and crying. How do we react? Perhaps we say, "Let's go do something else and get your mind off of this." But it would be better if we could enter her world of grief and feel with her and perhaps cry with her. Romans 12:15 states that we are to "weep with those who weep" (*NASB*).

Tears are all right. "We must not be ashamed of our tears," says Joyce Landorf. "Jesus wept on hearing of His friend Lazarus' death (even though He knew He was about to give Lazarus a remission from death!). To weep is not to be guilty of a lack of faith, nor is it a sign of hopelessness. Crying is a natural part of the grieving process."[6]

When grief is not expressed, there is a higher degree of what we call "psychosomatic reactions" such as ulcerated colitis, hypertension, etc. During the time of grief work, the bereaved may be irritable and you may notice some strained interpersonal relationships. This is normal.

The bereaved person needs three things:

1. Safe places. He needs his own home. Some people prefer to withdraw because their home reminds them of loss; but giving up the home and moving creates more of a loss. A brief change may be all right but familiar surroundings are more helpful.

2. Safe people. Friends, relatives, and a minister are necessary to give the person the emotional support he needs. If you are ministering to a bereaved person, it is better to visit the person four times a week for ten minutes than to come once a week for an hour. This provides more continual support without becoming exhaustive.

3. Safe situations. Any kind of safe situation that provides a bereaved person with worthwhile roles to perform benefits him. These situations should be uncomplicated and simple, and should not create anxiety. One pastor called at the home of a woman who had just lost her husband. He could tell that people had been coming in and out all day long and she was

tired of receiving them and their concern. As he came in he said, "You know, I've had a tiring day. Would it be too much to ask you to make a cup of tea or coffee for me?" She responded and fixed the coffee. When he was leaving she said, "Thank you for asking me to make you the coffee. I have started to feel worthwhile and useful again."

Perhaps what we need in order to be able to minister to others is a clear understanding of what death is. For the Christian death is a transition, a tunnel leading from this world into the next. Perhaps the journey is a bit frightening because we are leaving what security we can feel here and going to the unknown, but the final destination will be well worth the present uncertainty.

John Powell in *The Secret of Staying in Love* presents a beautiful description of the finality of life. "This book is gratefully dedicated to Bernice. She has been a source of support in many of my previous attempts to write. She has generously contributed an excellent critical eye, a cultivated literary sense and especially a confident kind of encouragement. She did not help with the preparation of this book. On July 11 she received a better offer. She was called by the Creator and the Lord of the Universe to join the celebration at the banquet of eternal life."[7]

Do men and women react the same way toward death? It seems not. Men seem to be more surprised at the fact of mortality than women. They sometimes react as though life had played a dirty trick on them. If a close friend or relative dies they can become preoccupied with the topic of death. They may even lose confidence in themselves and allow thoughts of death to cloud their efforts at work. Some men create an interesting illusion about life. They equate work success as a means of protecting themselves from the ravages of death. If we work hard and are successful it will drive both the thoughts and reality of death away and we gain a sense of immortality. One problem with this is that men tend to pursue one success after another in their flight from the fact of death. They never know when to stop. But in seeking success, after a time we discover that success cannot cover over our fears and in itself can actually create greater tension. And when disillusionment with work really hits during mid-life, as

Gould states, "we feel the cold breath of death on our own neck, we experience the demonic dread that it protected against."[8]

In order to guard against this fear many men work harder, longer, faster, more intensely and take on greater work loads. But eventually depression, strokes, ulcers and heart attacks may crowd into the picture and bring us face to face with what we have been trying to avoid all along—death.

Preparing for Your Own Death

You and I have no choice. We will die. But we can choose how we view death. We can also decide how we want to spend our remaining years; what to do with our body upon death; what we would like our funeral to reflect to those who attend; how we want others to remember us; where we would like to die if given a choice. We can learn to talk more openly about death, to fear death less, to anticipate how we would handle a terminal illness. We can determine whether or not we would allow ourselves to be kept alive on a machine. We can draw up a will and decide whether or not to carry life insurance.

You see, our faith does not spare us from physical death nor from the loss, hurt and pain of the grief process. It does offer us a hope of completion in the presence of Jesus.

At this point in life or in the near future you may experience the death of a parent, a close friend or your spouse. You may even soon face the prospect of your own dying; many know in advance that they are dying because they have some terminal disease. You cannot run from the death of another nor from your own death. You need to consider in advance what you will experience when you know you are dying. This will help you be better able to handle your inner turmoil and reactions. And if someone close to you is dying, knowing what he or she will experience will make you more able to minister. Some very predictable steps accompany the process of dying.

Dying means change. Even when we think we are prepared we still live with the fear that we will not be able to cope with our own death or that of another. We are afraid of the kinds of changes that will occur in us and what these changes will do to others.

Many people have greater fears and worries regarding the

process of dying than of death itself. A person with a terminal illness may worry about:

- being helpless
- being alone, deserted
- being dead, but no one notices
- pain and suffering
- being a burden (two-thirds of those in one study had this fear)
- humiliation (of being seen without his/her wig, dentures, or being unable to control bladder, etc.)
- what will happen to projects
- separation from loved ones
- the future for loved ones left behind
- eternal punishment
- physical impairment, of being unable to care for oneself
- the unknown
- others having to "take care of me"
- problems associated with finances
- loss of emotional control, of being "unable to take it."[9]

When a person discovers he is terminally ill, he experiences preparatory grief. This grief is important for it actually gives the individual some important and purposeful tasks to do while he is preparing himself and others for his death. It also helps those remaining to have less to do with the funeral arrangements. It helps the family learn to get along without him. This preparatory stage can lessen the sense of uselessness and helplessness which often occurs because he is actively preparing for his death. This preparatory grief can also minimize the loneliness of those left behind when he does die.

Accepting Death—Five Stages

When a person knows he is going to die, Dr. Kübler-Ross says that he usually experiences five different stages of emotional response.[10] His loved ones go through these same emotional reactions as well.

Stage 1: *Denial and isolation.* The first reactions are those of "It can't be. They're wrong. It's not me they are talking about." Some people make statements such as, "They'll find that someone in the lab made a mistake and then they'll come and tell me that I'll be all right." Or the person may go to doctor after doctor seeking another diagnosis and a new ray of hope. Not only does the person himself not want to hear that he will die, but the relatives and loved ones do not want to hear it either. The disciples didn't want to hear Jesus speak about His dying. Again and again He told them about His betrayal and crucifixion but they did not want to hear it.

Often a person experiences shock upon hearing the news. And one way in which shock manifests itself is through denial. Denial has been called the human shock-absorber to tragedy. Through denial our emotions are temporarily desensitized. Our sense of time is somewhat suspended because of our attempt to delay the consequences. Not only can the denial aspect of shock manifest itself in a reaction such as "Not me! No, I won't believe it," but in some cases denial can take the form of displaced concern. Some relatives who are shocked with the news about the loved one may try to act as though they are emotionally detached. But denial freezes the emotions and they must be thawed out eventually.

There are many ways in which one indicates that he/she is denying the inevitable. He:

- says he believes an error has been made by his doctor(s).
- explains disease symptoms as of another, less serious illness.
- says the doctor has promised quick restoration.
- never talks about death or dying; turns head away if dying is mentioned.
- talks constantly about plans for the future.
- openly says, "I don't believe it."
- seeks treatment through non-medical remedy or God's healing.
- never asks questions about the disease or its symptoms.
- refuses treatment, expecting symptoms to disappear by themselves.
- does not recognize drastic changes in physical appearance.
- speaks of treatment or hospitalization as of very short duration.
- talks of illness as minor.

- knows what the illness is but professes to be sure he will recover.
- explains reasons why he or she can't die yet. (God wouldn't be so cruel; my children need me; etc.)
- does not seem to hear questions or comments on illness.

"We need denial—but we must not linger in it," says author Joyce Landorf. "We must recognize it as one of God's most unique tools and use it. Denial is our special oxygen mask to use when the breath-taking news of death has sucked every ounce of air out of us. It facilitates our bursting lungs by giving them their first gulps of sorrow-free air. We breathe in the breath of denial and seem to maintain life. We do not need to feel guilty or judge our level of Christianity for clutching the mask to our mouth. However, after breathing has been restored and the initial danger has passed, we need not be dependent upon it.

"I think God longs for us to lay down the oxygen mask of denial, and with His help begin breathing into our lungs the fresh, free air of acceptance on our own."[11]

How can you help one who is in the denial stage? Don't judge him for what he is saying. No matter how difficult he seems or what he says, do not judge him. If the person is in the hospital do not expect too much response on the first, second, or even third visit. He may not feel like talking. Don't become discouraged and quit coming. Eventually he will respond because he needs someone with whom to share his loneliness. Perhaps the example we find in Job 2:13 can be a pattern for our response to such a person. "Then they sat upon the ground with him silently for seven days and nights, no one speaking a word; for they saw that his suffering was too great for words" (*TLB*).

Stage 2: *Anger.* A person confronted with death experiences anger, rage, envy, and resentment. "Why me, God? Why me? Why not someone else?" He may be angry at those around him who are well—friends, relatives, doctors. He is angry at the doctors who cannot make him well. He is angry at God for allowing this to happen and for not immediately healing him. In Job 7:11 (*TLB*) we read, "Let me be free to speak out of the bitterness of my soul." Perhaps this is what the person is experiencing at this point in his life. We may become the object of his anger simply because we are there. But we should not take the anger personally. Nor should we become judgmental and say he should not be angry. What he is experiencing is normal, part of the process. He may be demanding attention. Honest and open communication can help him feel understood.

Stage 3: *Bargaining.* "Spare me, Lord! Let me recover and be filled with happiness again before my death" (Ps. 39:13, *TLB*) is the prayer of so many people facing death. The person makes promises: "If I can get well then I will serve the Lord more than ever" or "If only I can live until June to see my son get married." Then, if he lives that long, he says, "If only I can live to see my grandchildren," and the process goes on and on.

This stage usually lasts only a brief period of time but it can be intense while it lasts. You may think, "If I were dying I wouldn't bargain." But you will. Hezekiah, a king in the Old Testament, was told by the Lord, "Set your affairs in order, for you are going to die; you will not recover from this illness" (Isa. 38:1 *TLB*). When he received the news he turned his face to the wall and bargained with God. He reminded God of how he had served and obeyed Him and then "broke down with great sobs" (38:3). In this instance Hezekiah's prayer was heard by God and he was given 15 more years to live. But God had a definite purpose.

Hezekiah's response to this experience is recorded in 38:17-20: "Yes, now I see it all—it was good for me to undergo this bitterness, for you have lovingly delivered me from death; you have forgiven all my sins. For dead men cannot praise you. They cannot be filled with hope and joy. The living, only the living, can praise you as I do today. . . . Think of it! The Lord healed me!"

The question arises, "Should we pray for complete healing for ourselves or another person?" It is certainly normal to want to be healed. Healing does occur, but it is not common. Family members bargain with God just as much as the terminally ill person. Perhaps our prayer ought to be for more pain-free moments for the person, for his complete knowledge of God's purpose and will, for the person's relationship to Christ to become stronger, and for the person's witness with the doctors, nurses, friends, and relatives.

Part of the bargaining process could reflect our own reaction to death and to God. We feel that God doesn't know what He is doing and we need to straighten Him out. Joe Bayly writes in *The View from the Hearse,* "Death for the Christian should be a shout of triumph, through sorrow and tears, bringing glory to God—not a confused misunderstanding of the will of God to heal."

Joyce Landorf shares the story of a lady who attempted to bargain with God. "She had lost her first husband after thirty years of marriage. Two years later she had married again and had seven happy years with a second husband. Then he got cancer.

"She told me they had been so very happy and the seven years had been so short that she pleaded and bargained with God to heal her husband. He was very close to dying and she knelt by his bed and begged the Lord to heal him so he wouldn't die. She said the Lord's voice spoke so clearly that she was quite startled by it. She heard Him say very distinctly in her mind, Your husband has prepared himself to accept death and to die right now. Tell Me, do you want him to prepare himself for death again—later on? She opened her eyes and looked at her husband—he was at peace—he had reached acceptance. She said, 'Oh Joyce, I knew right then I'd have to release him. I didn't want to make him go through that again—later on—so I released him. At that moment a great peace settled over me. He died a few hours later. Both of us were at peace.' If she had hung on, begged God to let her husband live, she would have missed what God wanted to do in their lives."[12]

Our ministry to the dying is to be a listener. James 1:19 in the *Amplified Version* says that we are to be "a ready listener." We are to listen but not give the dying person false hope. False reassurances do not help him, nor would they help us if we were in the same circumstance. Touching him and listening to him will show him that we care.

Stage 4: *Depression.* Denial does not work; anger does not work; bargaining does not work. And so the individual facing death concludes that nothing works, and depression sets in. This depression has two parts. One is called "reactive depression"—thinking about past memories—and the other is called "preparatory"—thinking about impending losses. This is a time when the person needs to pour out his sorrow. We can minister best at this point by sitting silently with the person or holding his hand and letting him know that it is all right to express his feelings. Don't argue or debate with him, for the consequences can only be negative.

Stage 5: *Acceptance.* The person now rests in the knowledge of what will happen. He has somewhat of a peaceful acceptance of his inevitable death. There is nothing else to do but accept the inevitable. The person may lose interest in most everything at this point and even become less talkative. We need to be honest with him and be truthful. He might ask how long he has to live. But we should never give a time limit as we never know for certain.

The family members probably need as much or more help and support as the dying person himself. They may not want him to know that he is terminally ill, but it is better for all concerned if he is told. The family members should be encouraged to face this crisis of life with the patient and not isolate him.

Abandonment Syndrome

One of the problems that can occur is the abandonment syndrome. Dying people express the fear that their condition will make them so unacceptable to others that they will be abandoned. In many cases studies have confirmed their fears. Some of the ways this abandonment occurs are as follows:

1. *A brief and formal monologue.* A relative or even a doctor may come in, ask a few rhetorical questions, and then leave without letting the person express his inner fears and hurts. People breeze in but seem to respond only on a superficial level. Some come in and inform the person how he ought to be feeling and promise to come back, but never return. What would you feel like if this were happening to you?

2. *Treating the person as though disease or accident has turned him into a nonperson.* He feels badly when others talk in front of him as though he were not there any longer. Even some unconscious persons can hear what is being said. Many who have survived a coma say that they heard the faithful, verbal prayers of others and they meant so much to them. We

should pray with the person whether or not we think he can hear us.

3. *Ignoring or rejecting the cues that the person attempts to give.* He may want to talk about what is happening. What would you say to the person who says, "I think I'm going to live on for many years"? That is a cue for you to level with him, to let him know that you know the truth. His feelings and how you interpret them are important to him.

4. *Literal abandonment.* Sometimes people in nursing homes, as well as terminally ill patients, are actually abandoned. Relatives say they "want to remember the person as he used to be," or "He receives better care at the home than we could give." Often this indicates a fear of death on the part of the relatives; they have to try to separate themselves from him in some way.

Another indication of abandonment—some loved ones initially have close contact with the terminally ill person such as kissing him on the lips. Then they begin to kiss him on the forehead, then the hand; and finally they simply blow a kiss from across the room. The patient can sense this form of rejection.

Where to Die?

Should the person return to his home to die? For some this may be best if he so desires. But others feel more comfortable staying at the hospital where they feel secure in an honest atmosphere and can receive good care.

For the Christian dying is a home-going. David Morley describes the journey for us so beautifully: "What a joyous moment that will be, when he will be reunited with all of his loved ones who have gone on before! When, once more, the lines of communication will be reestablished, the old voices heard again, and the deathly silence at last broken forever— no more goodbyes, no more quick slipping away of loved ones into the mysterious enigma of death.

"The most glorious anticipation of the Christian is that, at the time of death, he will come face-to-face with his blessed Lord, his wonderful, patient Redeemer, who all of those years continued to love him in spite of the countless times the man ignored Him and went his willful way. We will not be encountering a stranger, but the best and the most intimate friend that we have ever had. When we think of death as a time of revelation and reunion, we immediately remove its venom. We can say with the Apostle Paul, 'O death where is thy sting? O grave, where is thy victory?' (1 Corinthians 15:55)."[13]

Notes

1. Ernest Becker, *The Denial of Death* (New York: The Free Press, 1973), p. 215.
2. Joyce Landorf, *Mourning Song* (Old Tappan, NJ: Fleming H. Revell, 1974), p. 26.
3. J. William Worden and William Proctor, *Personal Death Awareness* (Englewood Cliffs, NJ: Prentice Hall Inc., 1976) pp. 11-16, adapted.
4. Granger Westberg, *Good Grief* (Philadelphia: Fortress Press, 1962), pp. 30-37.
5. Joshua Liebman, *Peace of Mind* (New York: Simon and Schuster, 1946), p. 109.
6. Landorf, *Mourning Song*, p. 147.
7. John Powell, *The Secret of Staying in Love* (Niles, IL: Argus Communications, 1974).
8. Roger Gould, *Transformations* (New York: Simon and Schuster, 1978), pp. 227,228, adapted.
9. Larry Richards and Paul Johnson, M.D., *Death and the Caring Community* (Portland, OR: Multnomah Press, 1980), p. 47.
10. Elizabeth Kübler-Ross, *On Death and Dying* (New York: Macmillan Company, 1969).
11. Landorf, *Mourning Song*, p. 63.
12. Ibid, pp. 83,84.
13. David C. Morley, *Halfway Up the Mountain* (Old Tappan, NJ: Fleming H. Revell, 1979), pp. 77,78.

Conclusion

You have reached your destination. A journey in your mind has just concluded. But no matter what your age you are still involved in life's journey. You may be just beginning or well on your way. At each stage of your marriage you, your partner and your relationship will be different. Part of the difference will occur because of the natural process of growth. Part will occur because of what you choose to do and the direction you give to your life and marriage.

You have something to say about the memories you are accumulating:

What will make the difference in the quality of your memories?

One word—commitment.

One word? Yes, but a costly word which can bring tension and questions at the same time it brings peace, maturity and stability.

In the midst of a life which brings rapid, unexpected changes, unfairness, tragedy and unanswered questions, commitment to living by faith will guide us through this journey.

Commit your life to the person of Jesus Christ who is the Son of God.

Commit your life to the Word of God which brings stability and peace.

Commit yourself to seeing your marriage partner as having such worth, value and dignity that God sent His Son to die for that person.

Commit your life as a couple to a life of prayer. There is no greater closeness and intimacy than when a couple opens their hearts to God together. Praying together enhances the completeness and oneness of a couple while it puts their differences and adjustments in a better perspective.

Commit your life to giving your marriage top priority in terms of time, energy, thought and planning for growth.

Commit yourself to a life of fidelity and faithfulness regardless of your feelings or the lure of life around you.

Commit and open yourself to the working of the Holy Spirit in your life. "But when the Holy Spirit controls our lives he will produce this kind of fruit in us: love, joy, peace, patience, kindness, goodness, faithfulness, gentleness, and self-control." Galatians 5:22,23, *TLB*